DAILY DEVOTIONS FOR KINGDOM SEEKERS

VOLUME III

DENNIS JERNIGAN

SHEPHERD'S HEART MUSIC

Published by Dennis Jernigan/Shepherd's Heart Music, Inc.

7804 West Fern Mountain

Muskogee, OK 74401

Jernigan, Dennis: Daily Devotions For Kingdom Seekers, Vol. 3

ISBNs: 978-1-948772-14-3 (paperback), 978-1-948772-13-6 (ebook)

Cover Design: Jones House Creative

HOW TO USE THIS BOOK

Over a decade ago, I started writing devotions to minister to my own soul. Each of these devotions, written in 2012, was born amidst my own struggles to seek first the King and His Kingdom. Through my spiritual journey, I have learned to walk in the reality of who I am in Christ. I have learned to walk in grace through any and every circumstance by incorporating a Kingdom point of view as the filter of my mind.

Because of all God has done for me, I want to help others find the same freedom and depth of intimacy with Christ I have come to know.

One thing to know about this book: each day's devotion begins with a phrase from one of my songs. Listen to the song daily. Memorize it. The words and melody will help you meditate, throughout the course of the day, on the truth of God's Word as revealed through each day's devotional reading. All songs can be found on Amazon Music, iTunes, Spotify, or at www.dennisjernigan.com. You can find the full list of songs in the Discography of this book.

Of course, you can read and apply the truths found in the devotionals without listening to the music. I have simply found *much* freedom from being able to sing a truth-filled song as I go about my day.

Above all, my desire is that this book would prove to be as useful a tool to your heart and soul as it was to mine in the writing. I have lived every word of this and can verify that seeking the King is the most profitable thing I can do with my life.

Now, go and be a Kingdom Seeker by seeking the King!

In His love & grace,
    Dennis Jernigan

JANUARY

JANUARY 1

"Great is Your faithfulness"

Listen to the song "Great is Your Faithfulness" from the album *The Worshipper's Collection, Vol 3.*

> *Great is Your faithfulness, Oh Lord! Oh Lord!*
> *Great is Your faithfulness, Oh Lord! Oh Lord!*
>
> *Great is Your faithfulness, Oh Lord! Oh Lord!*
> *Great is Your faithfulness, Oh Lord! Oh Lord!*
> *I've been hungry, yet, I never lack!*
> *For I see Your hand each time I look back!*
> *And I praise You for this very fact that I know!*
>
> *Great is Your faithfulness!*

Great is Your faithfulness!
Great is Your faithfulness!

Great is Your faithfulness, Oh Lord! Oh Lord!
Great is Your faithfulness, Oh Lord! Oh Lord!
Great is Your faithfulness, Oh Lord! Oh Lord!
I've been thirsty, yet, You send the rain!
I've been hurting, Lord, yet, You bore the pain!
And I praise You Whose love will sustain me

It can be amazing—the advantage of living enough years to look back on one's life. Older and wiser, one becomes more adept at seeing life from the King's point of view and, thus, becomes even more grateful. As we look back on past experiences and circumstances—both good and bad—we can either become bitter or glad. When one chooses to see from the Lord's perspective, joy replaces sorrow, hope replaces despair, forgiveness replaces bitterness, peace replaces anger, and life replaces death. *Someone* got us to where we are today. No matter how worn we are by the miles and road damage, we are *here* in this moment because of the mercy and goodness of the Lord.

Look back today and see your life from His point of view, and then thank Him often!

I will sing of the lovingkindness of the Lord forever;
   To all generations I will make known Your faithfulness with my mouth.

— PSALM 89:1

JANUARY 2

"Great is Your faithfulness"

God has been faithful whether we see His faithfulness or not. After all, if we got what we deserved, due to our sin, we would all be dead and in Hell! The enemy goes about doing his best to cloud our view of God's grace and mercy in our lives. We can choose to believe what the enemy shows us or we can choose to believe that our God is good and faithful. One way leads to bitterness and despair while the other leads to peace and hope regardless of our circumstances.

Spend time today focusing on the faithfulness of God. Ask the Holy Spirit to reveal ways you have missed seeing the hand of God in and upon your life, then thank Him for what He reveals!

> For I have said, "Lovingkindness will be built up forever; In the heavens You will establish Your faithfulness."
>
> — PSALM 89:2

JANUARY 3

"Great is Your faithfulness"

Have you ever felt alone? We all go through periods in life when we feel alone. Sometimes that feeling can permeate our thoughts even when we are in the midst of a crowd of people. What should that tell us? We are a relational being, created by

God for relationship with Him and with others. Relationship begets life. Life is meant to be lived abundantly. Even when we do not think so, God uses people in our lives to help get us to where we need to be. He is faithful that way!

Ask the Holy Spirit to remind you of some relationship that have helped get you to where you are. Thank God for them and consider thanking those people for the way God has used them in your life.

> For we are His workmanship, created in Christ Jesus for good works, which God prepared beforehand so that we would walk in them.

> — EPHESIANS 2:10

JANUARY 4

"Great is Your faithfulness"

When I was a boy, I felt very alone for many reasons, even though I was never physically alone. It was not until I was a grown man that the Lord began to reveal to me just how intricate and caring His faithfulness was to me. During a time of mental healing, He revealed to me that even during those alone times, He had engineered circumstances and people to guard over me.

My grandmother used to stand behind me and pray for me as I played the piano at her house. She died when I was 13. Years after she was gone, one of her friends told me how my grandmother would gather the women of her church each week to pray for me! When I heard that report, the years of hurt and wounding were flooded with feelings of care and love and protection. Even when so many hard things happened to me as a boy, God had been clearing the path to my healing for *years*!

Ask the Holy Spirit to guide you to places of discovering His previously unseen faithfulness to you today. Remember to thank Him for what He reveals!

> Let us hold fast the confession of our hope without wavering, for He who promised is faithful.

> — HEBREWS 10:23

JANUARY 5

"Oh Lord! Oh Lord"

When we hear the word *Lord* in a worldly sense, we usually attach a derogatory meaning to it—slumlord, warlord, or to lord one's authority over another. When I call Jesus my *Lord*, I am actually saying He is my sovereign King to Whom I yield the care of my life, along with yielding my life in service to Him. He is indeed a *good* Lord, not like the lords we see in the human race. This Lord wants only our best and, once we yield to His Lordship, uses even the messes we make of our lives to bring about our good.

I serve Him with my life because He served me with His. I bow before Him as my King because He willingly gave His life for mine. I follow Him because of the depth of love He passionately expressed on the cross to rescue me. He is Lord like no other, and I gladly yield to Him.

Take time to yield to the goodness of the Lord today.

That if you confess with your mouth Jesus as Lord, and believe in your heart that God raised Him from the dead, you will be saved.

— ROMANS 10:9

JANUARY 6

"I've been thirsty, yet You send the rain"

As I look back on my life, it is easy to see just how timely God's provision was. During the times when I thought I would lose my mind, someone saved my sanity with the right word spoken at the right time. When I felt utterly alone with no one to talk to about my darkest secrets, the Lord allowed someone with an amazing depth of grace to confront me with such love and hope that I could not resist the help offered. Just when I felt I would wither up and blow away from the sheer thirst of my soul, the Lord sent the rain I needed. Always. Although it sometimes seemed late coming, the beauty of hindsight allows us to see the bigger, broader picture of God's truth and reality.

Take time today to reflect on the many times God has proven His faithfulness in ways you had not seen at the time. Thank Him often throughout the day.

For as the rain and the snow come down from heaven,
And do not return there without watering the earth

And making it bear and sprout,

And furnishing seed to the sower and bread to the eater;

So will My word be which goes forth from My mouth;

It will not return to Me empty,

Without accomplishing what I desire,

And without succeeding in the matter for which I sent it.

— ISAIAH 55:10-11

JANUARY 7

"I've been hurting, Lord, yet You bore the pain"

At one point in my life, I remember feeling such unbearable pain of soul that I actually attempted to take my own life. As the gas hissed from the heating stove, I lay on the floor and gave up on God and on ever being free. I lay there, and a still, small voice came to my mind asking if I was prepared for what awaited me in eternity. After a few minutes, I turned off the gas. I walked in fear for the next few months.

Looking back, it is quite obvious that I had been visited by the Lord. And what is just as significant to me now: He was there bearing my pain *with* me.

To some degree, I experience my children's pain and sorrow, and—much to my delight—they allow me to help bear their pain and loss. If I, as an earthly father, can feel those things, how much *more* is our heavenly Father able to bear our pain and sorrow? A pain that is shared is a burden that is lightened.

Share your pain and sorrow with the Lord and another. See how those relationships lessen that pain and sorrow.

Surely our griefs He Himself bore,
And our sorrows He carried.

— ISAIAH 53:4A

JANUARY 8

"And I praise You Whose love will sustain me, I know"

Our Father loves us deeply, purely, and absolutely. When we believe we are unlovable, it's like telling God we know better than him! That is stinkin' thinkin'! To believe and receive the love of God is to empower ourselves to overcome *anything* in this life. *God's love conquers all!*

One of the quickest ways to put down the enemy and receive the love of God is to express our love in worship and praise. When we express our love to Father, we engage our entire being in focus on the Lord, and the enemy has no place to pin his lies because every part of our being is focused on Jesus!

When we believe God loves us, and unabashedly *receive* that love, we are sustained through the storms, chaos, fiery trials, sorrow, loss, and whatever else may come our way.

Spend time loving and being loved today, and watch your load be lightened.

Hatred stirs up strife,

But love covers all transgressions.

— PROVERBS 10:12

JANUARY 9

"Each day the desert grows harder"

Listen to the song "You Come Raining" from the album *Let It Rain.*

Each day the desert grows hotter
And relief is nowhere to see!
As a deer thirsts after the water
My soul, Lord, thirst after Thee!

When sin brings sorrow and suff'ring
To drown me in my own grief
I thirst for pure Living Water
And treasure each drop of relief!

You come raining,
My heart sustaining,
With wave upon wave of Your love
You sweep over me!

You come pouring,
My life restoring,
With showers and showers of rain in the desert!
O, rain on me!
Plunge me deep!

And carry me away!

Your love is great like a river
Whose pow'r and source have no end!
Like streams of life in the desert
Inviting me to plunge in!

With my heart adrift on this River
I want to lose all control!
My thirst is quenched in this River!
My life is drawn from the flow!

We've heard it said, "It always grows darkest just before the dawn," and have all experienced moments when that absolutely feels like the case. No matter how hard our life may become — no matter how hot, trying, and wearying the desert — we are never alone. We are never far from Living Water!

In any moment of life, we have instant and direct access to the Father through Jesus Christ, anywhere, anytime, under any circumstance! That is *amazing!* What do we have to fear if our God is that near?

Walk like you believe that today! Walk like you believe God is with you no matter what — whether you *feel* Him or not! Walk like the son or daughter of the Most High God that you are as a *new creation!* The new creation is equipped for any and every thing the enemy may throw our way. We but have to believe and receive!

Do not rejoice over me, O my enemy.
     Though I fall I will rise;
     Though I dwell in darkness, the Lord is a light for me.

— MICAH 7:8

10

"And relief is nowhere to see"

What role does faith play in our walk on this earth? Everything! Without faith, we do not have salvation. Without faith, we do not receive the power to overcome the lies of the enemy. Without simple faith, it is impossible to please God. But with one, small mustard seed of faith, we are saved, we are overcomers, and we are instantly pleasing to our Lord. All that without so much as one ounce of performing for His acceptance! Incredible!

This means that during times of trial and difficulty in life, we can find instant relief. By faith, we believe we are not alone and find that God is with us. By faith, we step toward the direction we feel God calling us and find ourselves walking on water. By faith, we find comfort from pain and sorrow by placing our trust and hope in God. Relief may not be visible to the naked, earthly eye, but to the eye of faith, it is *always* available!

Take time to step out in faith today and find relief in the process.

No temptation has overtaken you but such as is common to man; and God is faithful, who will not allow you to be tempted beyond what you are able, but with the temptation will provide the way of escape also, so that you will be able to endure it.

— 1 CORINTHIANS 10:13

JANUARY 11

"As a deer thirsts after the water"

As I write this, we are going through the longest, hottest spell since the early 1980s. We have not mown the lawn since spring and it is now mid-July. The grass is brown. The ponds are low. The people are lethargic and longing for cool weather and cooling, refreshing rain. We are thirsty in every sense of the word.

Last night we had a sudden rain shower, so I took off my shirt, put on my swim trunks and sat out *in* the rain! Even now, the next day, I see a rain shower heading our direction, hoping it makes it to our area. Even though these small showers do not do much for the land, they certainly have a refreshing effect on us as we remember how good the rain feels and how refreshing it is.

So it is with the Lord, and even more so. We long for Him expectantly and are so very grateful for every drop of His presence in the dry times of our lives.

Go about your day expecting His presence to surprise you in the dry times of your day. Then *enjoy* that rain!

As the deer pants for the water brooks,
So my soul pants for You, O God.
My soul thirsts for God, for the living God.

— PSALM 42:1-2A

JANUARY 12

"My soul, Lord, thirsts after Thee"

Thirst is a good thing. Thirst tells us our bodies needs water! Spiritual thirst leads us to the ultimate thing we need — Living Water! We often see thirst as negative, but without it, we would neglect putting life-giving water in our physical bodies. Just so, spiritual thirst — spurred on by dry times — is a *good* thing. If you are thirsting today, that is your spirit's clue to seek the Source of the water you need.

Seek Him in thought and search for evidence of His hand in all you do today. Seek Him and you will find Him. Seek to quench your thirst in Jesus today!

> You will seek Me and find Me when you search for Me with all your heart.
>
> — JEREMIAH 29:13

JANUARY 13

"When sin brings sorrow and suffering"

When I think about times of suffering in my life, the suffering of being victimized by others seems minimal compared to the suffering I brought upon myself by wrong choices — by sin. Far too often it is easier to blame God for our sorrow and suffering than to accept responsibility for our own choices. Even when we *are* victims of circumstances (a friend dies, a loved one betrays us, bad things happen to good people), we must place blame where blame is due: squarely on the back of sin. Sin brought death and despair into the world, not the Lord. Yes, He allowed it, but He knew that relationship requires a free will. He does not force us to love Him, and He does not force us to do right. He desires that we love Him just for Who He is—the same way He loves us!

Spend time today pondering these thoughts and allow the Holy Spirit to show you the big picture of sorrow and suffering. Take time to rejoice in His redemptive plan for you.

> And we know that God causes all things to work together for good to those who love God, to those who are called according to His purpose.

> — ROMANS 8:28

JANUARY 14

"To drown me in my own grief"

Grief is a natural part of the healing process. When we recognize this fact we are more apt to accept God's healing hand of recovery in that process. Far too often, I allow myself to focus where the enemy wants me to focus rather than on the Kingdom picture where God wants me to focus. Death comes to someone I love—or to a vision or dream—and all I see is the loss. As long as the loss is my focus, the enemy has me in his vile grip. When I choose to allow the Lord to lead me to His point of view, I am taken on a wondrous journey called healing that I would not have experienced otherwise. Did I lose something dear? Of course. Is that the end of the world? Not at all. I will see the loved one again in time. God will give me bigger and better visions and dreams because He desires to bless His children, and I am one of His children!

Sorrowing today? Own it, but walk it out *with* Father.

Gracious is the Lord, and righteous;
    Yes, our God is compassionate.
    The Lord preserves the simple;
    I was brought low, and He saved me.

— PSALM 116:5

JANUARY 15

"I thirst for pure Living Water"

When I am thirsty my thirst is never fully quenched by substitutes for water. Coke leaves me feeling weird. Alcohol would numb my senses. Drinking sand would never work! Only the real thing satisfies *really*. Just as with our physical body, the thirst of our soul is never fully satisfied by anything other than the *real* thing — pure Living Water. The good news is that we have constant and instant access to that Water because we are in a living, thriving relationship with *the* Source, Jesus Christ!

Spend time seeking Him today. Spend time allowing your thirst to lead you to Him today. Satisfy yourself as deeply and as often as necessary. Just cry out to Him from the thirsty places in your soul.

O God, You are my God; I shall seek You earnestly;
My soul thirsts for You, my flesh yearns for You,
In a dry and weary land where there is no water.
Thus I have seen You in the sanctuary,
To see Your power and Your glory.
Because Your lovingkindness is better than life,
My lips will praise You.
So I will bless You as long as I live;
I will lift up my hands in Your name.
My soul is satisfied as with marrow and fatness,
And my mouth offers praises with joyful lips.

— PSALM 63:1-5

JANUARY 16

"And treasure each drop of relief"

Isn't it wonderful to be able to look back on our lives and see just how far the Lord has brought us from where we once were in our sin? This gives us hope for our current difficulties and harsh circumstances. If God has gotten us through before, will He not get us through once again? When in a desert, we should learn to treasure even the smallest relief—a bit of morning dew, a brief respite of shade under a wilting tree. When in a storm, we should learn to treasure the Anchor to which we are attached. It holds fast even when the waves beat relentlessly and the winds blow in howling ferocity. A heart of gratitude goes a long way in hard times.

Look around for the treasures of God's provision and presence—no matter how small they appear to you—and thank

Him in the midst of the desert, in the midst of the storm, and find your heart lifted in the process.

You have heard my voice,
"Do not hide Your ear from my prayer for relief,
From my cry for help."
You drew near when I called on You;
You said, "Do not fear!"

— LAMENTATIONS 3:56-57

JANUARY 17

"You come raining"

As of this writing, we are in the midst of summer without any rain. Today marks day 19 of over 100 degree weather! We have not had to mow the lawn all summer. The corn crop next to us will be a total loss for the farmer. Everyone seems lethargic, and outdoor work is miserable. It is during times like this that we long for even a brief shower of rain, or the few second's worth of shade offered by the rare, passing cloud.

Yet, we have plenty of water. We have shelter from the heat. We have food on the table. We have our friends and families to bolster our spirits with the laughter and tears sweet fellowship always brings. Even though we are in a drought with unbearable heat, God still blesses. We *must* learn to see from the King's perspective during the dry times or we will walk around in defeat and in misery. That is no way for a servant of the King to live!

Choose to see what God sees in the midst of your circumstances. Live an *abundant* life as you enjoy the feast of His presence laid out right before you.

> For as the rain and the snow come down from heaven,
> And do not return there without watering the earth
> And making it bear and sprout,
> And furnishing seed to the sower and bread to the eater;
> So will My word be which goes forth from My mouth;
> It will not return to Me empty,
> Without accomplishing what I desire,
> And without succeeding in the matter for which I sent it.

— ISAIAH 55:10-11

JANUARY 18

"My heart sustaining"

Sometimes, life has a way of keeping us so busy that we lose sight of the shore. Sometimes, the enemy and his lies bombard us to the point that we feel like we are losing our ability to see the truth. In either scenario, the truth is what we must always get back to. When to the intensity of our schedule makes us lose sight of the shore, we must speak to the winds of our minds and say, "Peace, be still," and refocus our attention on what truly matters—our God and our purpose in life. When we feel overwhelmed by the lies of the enemy, we must speak to that onslaught as well, saying, "Get behind me, Liar. I am who my Father says I am!" In refocusing our thoughts, we take back any ground the enemy may have stolen from under our feet. By putting off lies and putting on truth, we put *him* under our feet where he belongs, take our thoughts captive and, once again, walk in the feast of God's presence and truth.

Take time to re-focus your thoughts, right now!

> For though we walk in the flesh, we do not war according to the flesh, for the weapons of our warfare are not of the flesh, but divinely powerful for the destruction of fortresses. We are destroying speculations and every lofty thing raised up against the knowledge of God, and we are taking every thought captive to the obedience of Christ, and we are ready to punish all disobedience, whenever your obedience is complete.

> — 2 CORINTHIANS 10:3-6

JANUARY 19

"With wave upon wave of Your love You sweep over me"

I will never forget the moment I absolutely realized that God loves me. Growing up in the church had not kept me immune from the lies of the Liar. The Enemy had me convinced that I was unlovable! During a time of worship (30 years ago now!), I was challenged to allow the Lord to take my greatest failures, disappointments, wounds, and sin, and *let* Him love me! I'd been deciding if and when God could love me for so long that I'd *kept* Him from lavishing His love on me. The truth broke through my messed up mind and showed me that not only did God love me *right where I was*, but that He loved me enough *to not leave me there!* It was as if I was sitting in the surf of a cool, refreshing beach and wave upon wave of His love swept over me. That was 30 years ago, and the waves have not stopped!

Let God love you today. He has forgiven you. Have you forgiven yourself? Let Him love you, and do not set any limits on that love.

> And you were dead in your trespasses and sins, in which you formerly walked according to the course of this world, according to the prince of the power of the air, of the spirit that is now working in the sons of disobedience. Among them we too all formerly lived in the lusts of our flesh, indulging the desires of the flesh and of the mind, and were by nature children of wrath, even as the rest. But God, being rich in mercy, because of His great love with which He loved us, even when we were dead in our transgressions, made us alive together with Christ (by grace you have been saved), and raised us up with Him, and seated us with Him in the heavenly places in Christ Jesus, so that in the ages to come He might show the surpassing riches of His grace in kindness toward us in Christ Jesus.
>
> — EPHESIANS 2:1-7

JANUARY 20

"You come pouring"

I believe we can have as much of the Lord as we desire in this life. By that I mean this: relationship is everything, and if we do not work at relationship we actually diminish our capacity for life, for *abundant* life. If I withhold my emotions and my words and my actions from my wife, our relationship suffers and eventually dies. But when I *give* myself in every possible way, life actually *flourishes*! For me to try and reserve a part of me is to deny her full access to my heart. It is no different in our relationship with the Lord. He freely gives Himself to us. We are to freely give ourselves to Him. When we stop putting Him in a box—and stop putting ourselves in a box—we effectively take off any limitations in that relationship. Nothing hidden means life can flow freely! God pours Himself out freely upon us, are we ready to receive?

Pour yourself out on Him today, and be ready for a flood of love and grace and glory from Him!

Trust in Him at all times, O people;
Pour out your heart before Him;
God is a refuge for us. Selah.

— PSALM 62:8

JANUARY 21

"My life restoring"

God's idea of restoration is much greater than our limited point of view. When we think restoration, we think of getting back what we lost. When the Lord thinks restoration, He thinks of taking us far beyond where we were and of giving us more than we can humanly conceive! When I think of my life and where I used to be, why would I *ever* want to go *back*? That would be ludicrous! Even in times of great loss, I have learned to allow the Lord to show me His plan for restora-

21

tion; it *always* exceeds my feeble attempts to figure everything out.

We can either allow the loss of our lives to be our focus or we can allow the Lord to bring restoration and carry us to heights of freedom and victory we have only dreamed. Just as we do not limit God, we must not limit ourselves from receiving all He offers us in the process of restoration. Think outside the box today!

> Then I will make up to you for the years
> > That the swarming locust has eaten,
> > The creeping locust, the stripping locust and the gnawing
> locust,
> > My great army which I sent among you.
> > You will have plenty to eat and be satisfied
> > And praise the name of the Lord your God,
> > Who has dealt wondrously with you;
> > Then My people will never be put to shame.
> > Thus you will know that I am in the midst of Israel,
> > And that I am the Lord your God,
> > And there is no other;
> > And My people will never be put to shame.

> — JOEL 2:25-27

JANUARY 22

"With showers and showers of rain in the desert"

Often, we go without the things we need simply because we are too proud to make our needs known. Which of us would deny assistance if we saw someone fallen and in pain? We would readily do for others, yet we pridefully refuse to ask for help ourselves! Very much of the time, we have not, because we ask not! As we know, without relationship there would be no life, physically or spiritually. Without communicating our needs, how will those needs be met? That leaves us to our own devices, and how did that work out for you when you were lost in sin?

Make your requests known to the Lord and to others, and stand back in amazement at the creative ways our God meets your needs today.

> You do not have because you do not ask. You ask and do not receive, because you ask with wrong motives.
>
> — JAMES 4:2B-3A

JANUARY 23

"Oh, rain on me"

Isn't it a wonderful feeling to see a friend or relative after quite some time and to run into one another's arms? That exuberant embrace feels like complete joy and satisfaction because what was longed for is finally realized. When we go through long periods of spiritual or emotional dryness, we long for the Lord to embrace us with His arms of love. Sometimes that dryness takes the form of "Why am I here?" or "What am I doing with my life?" Rather than focusing on the dryness, it is better to drink deeply from the oasis of the Lord's presence that reminds us, "You are here for *My* purposes, child. Learn of

Me and find meaning and joy in all you do." Drink deep today and allow the Lord to remind you why you are here. Then thank Him!

> And we know that God causes all things to work together for good to those who love God, to those who are called according to His purpose.

> — ROMANS 8:28

JANUARY 24

"Plunge me deep"

Why do we so often settle for the shallow things of life? Could it be because we do not want to put in the work required to go deeper? After all, the shallow end of the pool is fun for awhile, but the joy of plunging into the deep end requires that we move, and come up for air, and continue to swim! I do not want to settle for the shallows in my relationship with the Lord or with others. The joy of relating to the Lord and others in a healthy manner is always worth our time and effort.

Let us focus today on doing the work required to go deeper.

> "Everything, O king, Araunah gives to the king." And Araunah said to the king, "May the Lord your God accept you." However, the king said to Araunah, "No, but I will surely buy it from you for a price, for I will not offer burnt offerings to the Lord my God which cost me nothing." So David bought the threshing floor and the oxen for fifty

shekels of silver. David built there an altar to the Lord and offered burnt offerings and peace offerings. Thus the Lord was moved by prayer for the land, and the plague was held back from Israel.

— 2 SAMUEL 24:23-25

JANUARY 25

"And carry me away"

Most of us do not have the luxury of dropping everything and getting away from all the chaos of life. Yet, in a spiritual sense, we can do just that! I have learned to meditate on the Word of the Lord and to talk with Him even in a crowd, which means I can take little spiritual *getaways* even when under duress! God's Word tells us we can take *every* thought captive. Meditation helps train our minds to do just that.

Let us focus today on this simple passage of Scripture and begin transforming our minds to get away whenever we need to!

For though we walk in the flesh, we do not war according to the flesh, for the weapons of our warfare are not of the flesh, but divinely powerful for the destruction of fortresses. We are destroying speculations and every lofty thing raised up against the knowledge of God, and we are taking every thought captive to the obedience of Christ.

— 2 CORINTHIANS 10:3-5

"Your love is great like a river"

Today, let us get a bigger vision of God's love for us. Due to our past failures (sin) and the wounds we have received at the hands of other wounded people, we often see the love of God through a skewed filter. Let us take God and His love *out* of that box, and let us view God's love as a mighty river, powerful and unending. See His capacity to love us as an unleashed deluge of power and grace that flows from that mighty river into an endless and unbounded ocean of sheer love.

Today, Drink deep. Plunge deep. Enjoy the flow and allow it to carry you *over* the circumstances of life.

How blessed is the man who does not walk in the counsel of
the wicked,
    Nor stand in the path of sinners,
    Nor sit in the seat of scoffers!
    But his delight is in the law of the Lord,
    And in His law he meditates day and night.
    He will be like a tree firmly planted by streams of water,
    Which yields its fruit in its season
    And its leaf does not wither;
    And in whatever he does, he prospers.

— PSALM 1:1-3

JANUARY 27

"Whose power and source know no end"

Why do we ever allow the enemy to put limits on the Lord and His love and His power? It happens every time we take our eyes away from the King and stop seeing from His point of view. When we do that, we see only the limiting, debilitating chaos and circumstances of life. It is when we begin to feel overwhelmed that we, rather than focus on the circumstances, must force our eyes back to the King and begin—even in the midst of that trial—to see what *He* sees. From that vantage point, we see that His power and ability to meet us anywhere, anytime, are boundless.

Focus on the Source of boundless love today!

For indeed He was crucified because of weakness, yet He lives because of the power of God. For we also are weak in Him, yet we will live with Him because of the power of God directed toward you.

— 2 CORINTHIANS 13:4

JANUARY 28

"Like streams of life in the desert"

As I write this, we are experiencing a record-breaking heat wave. We've had temperatures of over 100 degrees for over a month now. Adding to the heat is the drought. It seems there is no end in sight. Though we have had brief showers a few times, the ground is cracked and parched. Stepping outside on a day when the temperature is 115 degrees is like a slap in the face. It takes one's physical breath away. When we experience circumstances of life that make us feel like we are in an unending drought of the soul, we must take the necessary actions to sustain and preserve our lives. We have rivers and lakes to plunge into, but we must make an effort to go *to* those places of refuge. We must do the same in our souls.

Today, let us make the effort necessary to quench our thirst. By faith, step boldly into the oasis of His presence, drink long, and plunge deep!

Do not call to mind the former things,
　　Or ponder things of the past.
　　Behold, I will do something new,
　　Now it will spring forth;
　　Will you not be aware of it?
　　I will even make a roadway in the wilderness,
　　Rivers in the desert.

— ISAIAH 43:18-19

JANUARY 29

"Inviting me to plunge in"

Knowing Jesus means we are in a wonderful, open, always available relationship. As new creations, the only reason we don't experience His presence is that we either refuse to acknowledge Him or we do not make the effort to step into His presence. Even when I have gone through periods when I did not have the mental strength to acknowledge Him, it was when I made the simple effort to confess my weakness *to* Him that He met me there instantaneously!

Today, let us boldly plunge into His presence for the sheer joy of knowing Him and being known by Him!

> How great are Your works, O Lord!
> Your thoughts are very deep.

> — PSALM 92:5

JANUARY 30

"With my heart adrift on this river I want to lose all control"

Doesn't it sometimes seem that our lives are being controlled by our circumstances? Bills need to be paid now. Kids need to be driven here and there now. Our work requires that we be at that meeting now. Our spouse needs our attention now. On and on and on it seems to go. How do we stop the madness of feeling out of control? We must learn to plunge into the River of Life by faith, even in the midst of our busy schedules. Easier said than done, but it *is* possible.

We can prioritize our lives and learn to say no. Just because something is urgent does not mean it requires your attention *right now*. What *is* important is your spiritual well-being. As we learn to meditate on the Lord and focus on Him we begin to see life from His perspective and, in the process, place our hearts and minds squarely in the peaceful flow of that River, even while life rages on!

Spend time in the River today.

For thus says the Lord, "Behold, I extend peace to her like a
river,
    And the glory of the nations like an overflowing stream"

— ISAIAH 66:12A

JANUARY 31

"My thirst is quenched in this river"

We can try to satisfy our needs through our own strength
and the ways of the world, but those things were never meant
to bring complete satisfaction. We were created to have fellowship with God. It is when we learn to allow Him to meet our
needs that we experience true satisfaction.

Today, enjoying knowing that He is with You and wants to
meet each and every need of your life, whether physical,
emotional, or mental. He is able. Trust Him.

Trust in the Lord with all your heart
    And do not lean on your own understanding.
    In all your ways acknowledge Him,
    And He will make your paths straight.

— PROVERBS 3:5-6

FEBRUARY

FEBRUARY 1

"My life is drawn from the flow"

Since the Lord is our Creator and the Giver of Life, we are foolish to try and find our life through any other means or source. To try and find life through sex, drugs, or rock and roll, to quote an old cliché', is equivalent to a pumpkin deciding to detach itself from the vine and seek out its own source of sustenance and life. Soon enough, that gourd would wither and die in its own strength. Our lives are no different. He is our source. We must stay connected to Him to survive—for *abundant* life.

Spend time nurturing that connection today. Just ask Him what He's thinking about you!

Abide in Me, and I in you. As the branch cannot bear fruit of itself unless it abides in the vine, so neither can you unless you abide in Me. I am the vine, you are the branches; he who abides in Me and I in him, he bears much fruit, for apart from Me you can do nothing.

— JOHN 15:4-5

~

FEBRUARY 2

"Great is Your faithfulness, O Lord! O, Lord"

Let us take the time today to focus—all day long—on all God has done for us in our past. Let us recall the former calamities he rescued us from. Let us remember the former states of depravity we were redeemed from. Let us bring to remembrance each and every time His provision came or we realized His protection just in the nick of time.

Make today a day of thanksgiving and gratitude to the One who got us here!

God is faithful, through whom you were called into fellowship with His Son, Jesus Christ our Lord.

— 1 CORINTHIANS 1:9

~

FEBRUARY 3

"Great is Your faithfulness, O Lord! O, Lord"

Just as we spent time thanking God for his faithfulness in our past yesterday, let us use today to meditate on our present needs and thank Him before we even see His provision. He sees before we see. He puts the process of provision in motion before we ever even see the need.

Let us be like our Father today and thank Him *ahead* of time. It will build your faith and keep your eyes focused on Christ and the needs of others. Thank Him all day long!

> It will also come to pass that before they call, I will answer; and while they are still speaking, I will hear.
>
> — ISAIAH 65:24

FEBRUARY 4

"I've been hungry yet I never lack"

We all go through periods of hunger. We hunger to under-stand the meaning of our existence. We hunger to know more of God. We hunger to see loved ones we have not seen in a long while. We hunger to know others and to be known. We hunger for physical food. Hunger is a *good* thing! If we did not hunger, we would not eat, and if we did not eat, we would die! As it goes physically, so it goes spiritually. We all hunger to know God whether we recognize that hunger or not. He is eager to feed His sheep, but we must be willing to seek what He prepares for us. Our times of lacking should serve to stir us to action, not to wait to be spoon-fed!

Seek Jesus today and feast on His abundant presence.

Jesus said to them, "I am the bread of life; he who comes to Me will not hunger, and he who believes in Me will never thirst."

— JOHN 6:35

FEBRUARY 5

"For I see Your hand each time I look back"

Let us take some time today to reflect on times when the Lord has specifically answered a prayer or met a need. When we go through periods of intense need or lack, we tend to forget what God has already done because of the present pressure we are under. That pressure, and the lies of the enemy, can be put aside when faced with the truth that God provides for His children.

Even if you are not in need today, it is always good to look back and give thanks for all He has done. The heart of gratitude always leads to a better attitude!

Only fear the Lord and serve Him in truth with all your heart; for consider what great things He has done for you.

— 1 SAMUEL 12:24

FEBRUARY 6

"And I praise You for this very fact that I know"

Today is a good day to praise the Lord, in spite of what you lack. A Kingdom point of view reminds us of what we *do* have. We have an ever-present Friend who will hear our pleas anytime, anywhere. We have a Father who loves us right where we are but who loves us enough to not leave us there. We have One who defends us against the Liar. We have One who constantly serves us and lays down His life for us, leading us to a deeper and better understanding of who and of whose we are. We have One who always leads us to greater freedom —higher up and further in!

Praise Him for what you have been given today. You're alive! You have purpose! You are wanted!

The LORD is my strength and my shield;
My heart trusts in Him, and I am helped;
Therefore my heart exults,
And with my song I shall thank Him.

— PSALM 28:7

FEBRUARY 7

"Great is Your faithfulness"

Let us think back on our lives to the point where we felt lost and hopeless and in need of a Savior. Remember how faithful He was in spite of your lack of faithfulness to Him. Remember the work of the cross. Remember the blood shed just for you. Remember the power of the resurrection made available to you. Remember and be grateful. Give thanks.

> For God has not given us a spirit of timidity, but of power and love and discipline. Therefore do not be ashamed of the testimony of our Lord or of me His prisoner, but join with me in suffering for the gospel according to the power of God, who has saved us and called us with a holy calling, not according to our works, but according to His own purpose and grace which was granted us in Christ Jesus from all eternity.
>
> — 2 TIMOTHY 1:7-9

FEBRUARY 8

"Great is Your faithfulness"

Today, why don't we spend time thanking God for his faithfulness as expressed through the people has brought into our lives along the journey of faith—a parent, a coach, a teacher, a friend, an aunt or uncle, a random stranger. Allow the Holy Spirit to take you outside the obvious and remind you of peripheral relationships or forgotten people you knew only briefly. God always uses people to bless people. Thank Him for those He brings to mind, and then consider sending a note or card of thanks to those individuals.

But if we walk in the Light as He Himself is in the Light, we

have fellowship with one another, and the blood of Jesus His
Son cleanses us from all sin.

— 1 JOHN 1:7

FEBRUARY 9

"Great is Your faithfulness"

Sometimes the Lord engineers circumstances and events to
help us see His guiding hand, and often, we simply don't see
such things as anything more than mere coincidence. Looking
back on your life, are there any specific circumstances that
come to mind that you now see were the Lord's hand reaching
directly into your life? Thank Him for those moments, and
open your heart and mind to see the bigger picture from *His*
point of view. He is more interactive in our lives than we ever
give Him credit for. Let's begin to change that!

And we know that God causes all things to work together for
good to those who love God, to those who are called
according to His purpose.

— ROMANS 8:28

FEBRUARY 10

"Great is Your faithfulness! Oh Lord! Oh Lord!"

Our God has the ability to take even the things the Liar

intended as evil and turn those things into something good and beautiful and life-giving. He is able to restore what the devouring locusts have eaten from our bounty. He is able to bring forth beauty from the ashes our sin has left us in. He is able to take the little we offer and produce a bountiful feast right in the midst of our enemies.

Spend time today thanking Him for the times in your life He has done just that. Today will be a glorious day as we fill it with such powerful, holy thoughts.

The Spirit of the Lord God is upon me,
    Because the Lord has anointed me
    To bring good news to the afflicted;
    He has sent me to bind up the brokenhearted,
    To proclaim liberty to captives
    And freedom to prisoners;
    To proclaim the favorable year of the Lord
    And the day of vengeance of our God;
    To comfort all who mourn,
    To grant those who mourn in Zion,
    Giving them a garland instead of ashes,
    The oil of gladness instead of mourning,
    The mantle of praise instead of a spirit of fainting.
    So they will be called oaks of righteousness,
    The planting of the Lord, that He may be glorified.

— ISAIAH 61:1-3

FEBRUARY 11

"I've been thirsty, yet You send the rain"

In the same way that we would die if we did not hunger and seek food, we will die even more quickly if we try to go without water. Jesus calls Himself the *Living* Water. This water never runs dry and is always available to the new creation. Even when we experience dry times of the soul He is with us to give us life-sustaining drinks of His presence.

What do you thirst for today? Seek sustaining drinks from the presence of the Lord today.

He who believes in Me, as the Scripture said, "From his innermost being will flow rivers of living water."

— JOHN 7:38

FEBRUARY 12

"I've been hurting, Lord, yet You bore the pain"

There is nothing new under the sun. Even the pain we go through in life, someone else has gone through. That is not to negate our pain or to say it is not valid or important, it just means that we are not alone, and someone — Someone — understands. When pain is shared, the load is lessened and healing can begin.

Whatever pain or sorrow you are feeling today, know that Jesus bore it on the cross for you and is with you *through* it right now. In sheer honesty, confess your pain to Him and allow Him to bring comfort to your soul. If you are not in spiritual, emotional, or physical pain today, minister to someone who is.

> Surely our griefs He Himself bore,
> And our sorrows He carried;

— ISAIAH 53:4A

FEBRUARY 13

"And I praise You whose love will sustain me, I know"

When we praise the Lord in spite of how we feel and in spite of our circumstances, our focus is taken away from whatever the enemy—the Liar—wants us to focus on. When we praise God, we effectively take dominion over our own thoughts, attitudes, and actions. When we simply choose to acknowledge God's presence, love, and power in our lives, our entire being becomes infused with hope, faith, grace, and all that God is.

Let us spend the day praising God for all His benefits and his wonderful presence in our lives.

> Praise the Lord!
> Oh give thanks to the Lord, for He is good;
> For His lovingkindness is everlasting.

— PSALM 106:1

"Praise Him in the heavens"

Listen to the song "Praise Him In The Heavens" from the album *We Are The Army*.

Praise Him in the heavens!
Praise Him in the heights!
Praise Him all ye angels
And the stars of purest light!

Praise Him all ye nations!
Sounding this decree!
Jesus is Almighty God!
And Lord of All is He!

He is Lord!
Praise His name!
Sing hallelujah!
To the name of Jesus!

He is Lord!
Praise His name!
Sing hallelujah!
Christ is Lord!

Praise Him for His goodness!
His righteousness and might!
Praise Him for His faithfulness
And glory shining bright!

Praise the Holy Spirit,
Father, and the Son!
Praise unto Almighty God!
The Lord of All is One!

How do we praise Him in the heavens? The angels magnify the Lord around the throne. Their attitude is one of praise and adoration. Yet we have even more reason to praise God: we have been redeemed! We praise Him with a heavenly attitude when we acknowledge the Lord's many attributes and goodness toward us, and when we acknowledge the great things He has done for us. To praise Him like this is to join in with the heavenly hosts.

Remember your redemption today and praise Him more loudly than the angels!

Praise the Lord! Praise the Lord from the heavens.

— PSALM 148:1A

FEBRUARY 15

"Praise Him in the heights"

What are the high places in your life? What are the vistas you now view because of the Lord's goodness that you could not see even a year ago? What are the low places He has brought you out of? Praise Him today for all He has done to take you from the lowest of lows to the highest of highs. Praise

Him regardless of how you feel. Meditate on His greatness and on the great things He has done for you!

Praise Him in the heights!

— PSALM 148:1B

FEBRUARY 16

"Praise Him all ye angels and the stars of purest light"

Angels are messengers of God, and God has given angels charge over us to guide and protect. But we can join them in another of their heavenly charges—to heap praise on the Lord! Join with the angels in praising God today. As night approaches, set aside time to step out into the darkness and look up at the night sky. Just as numerous as the stars are, let our praise and honor of God be that glorious tonight. Praise Him with the angels through the day, and thank God with the stars as they testify of His massive greatness!

Praise Him, all His angels;
  Praise Him, all His hosts!
  Praise Him, sun and moon;
  Praise Him, all stars of light!

— PSALM 148:2-3

*"Praise Him all ye nations sounding this decree, 'Jesus is
Almighty God and Lord of all is He!'"*

Whether or not the world rises up and praises God, all of
creation will one day do that very thing. Every knee will bow
and every tongue will confess to the Lordship of Jesus Christ.
As new creations—as Kingdom Seekers—we do not have to
wait until *one day*! We can enter into that glory in the here and
now simply by a step of faith.

Step out in faith today and praise God in spite of your
circumstances and in spite of how you feel. Confess the Lordship of Jesus Christ and give God the glory due His name!

Praise Him, highest heavens,
  And the waters that are above the heavens!
  Let them praise the name of the Lord,
  For He commanded and they were created.

— PSALM 148:4-5

FEBRUARY 18

"He is Lord! Praise His name!"

Whether we choose to believe it or not does not alter the
fact that Jesus Christ is Lord! He is Lord even when we face
trials. He is Lord even when we are grieving. He is Lord even
when the world around us seems to be out of control. When we

step out in faith and acknowledge the Lordship of Jesus Christ, we effectively get into the universal flow of God's plan and power and glory. Like a mighty river that flows unhindered by the plans of men, the power of God is evident when we choose to see with Kingdom perspective. Spend time today seeing beyond what the enemy wants you to see. Praise his name and proclaim Him Lord in both word and deed.

> These will wage war against the Lamb, and the Lamb will overcome them, because He is Lord of lords and King of kings, and those who are with Him are the called and chosen and faithful.
>
> — REVELATIONS 17:14

FEBRUARY 19

"Sing alleluia to the name of Jesus!"

The word *alleluia* literally means "praise the Lord." There is a specialness to that word. It is understood in virtually every language on earth. When we say *alleluia* in praise to God, we are, in a way, joining with all mankind wherever that word is uttered. There is power in *alleluia* because it invokes the power of God by filling our souls with the awareness that God is with us. When we praise God, we give Him a place to sit, making our heart a throne for Him.

Use *alleluia* in outward demonstration of praise today as you drive to work or sip your coffee and read the paper! Just praise Him!

Then I heard something like the voice of a great multitude and like the sound of many waters and like the sound of mighty peals of thunder, saying, "Hallelujah! For the Lord our God, the Almighty, reigns."

— REVELATION 19:6

~

FEBRUARY 20

"Sing alleluia Christ is Lord!"

Continue praising God today by using the simple, anointed word *alleluia* as a launching point. Acknowledge the Lordship of Christ with your words, with your thoughts, with you attitudes, and with your actions. Declare His Lordship louder than words can convey by living your life in such a way that there is absolutely no doubt Jesus is Lord!

For this reason also, God highly exalted Him, and bestowed on Him the name which is above every name, so that at the name of Jesus every knee will bow, of those who are in heaven and on earth and under the earth, and that every tongue will confess that Jesus Christ is Lord, to the glory of God the Father.

— PHILIPPIANS 2:9-11

FEBRUARY 21

"Praise Him for His goodness"

At times, it is difficult to see the goodness of the Lord, like when a child dies, when a war breaks out, when terrorists keep an entire nation in fear, when bad things happen to good people. God is perfect in every way—including goodness. To not acknowledge His goodness gives place for the enemy to plant the debilitating seeds of his lies. And when his lies replace the truth of God, nothing good is going to come of that. Yet God—in His massive goodness—can take even the moments we believe the lies of the enemy and fall into evil and bring about good in our lives! Amazing!

God is good. Acknowledge His goodness throughout the day today.

> Surely God is good to Israel,
>   To those who are pure in heart!

— PSALM 73:1

FEBRUARY 22

"His righteousness and might"

If we had to rely on our own righteousness to be saved, we would be doomed. If we had to rely on our own strength and might to overcome, we would be faced with utter weakness. The great news is that we are saved by the righteousness of

Jesus Christ and we overcome the enemy by the power of His might! You, as a new creation, are a prince or princess of the Kingdom. His righteousness is *yours*! His power is *yours*!

Believe that truth, receive it, and walk like a child of the King!

> For all have sinned and fall short of the glory of God, being justified as a gift by His grace through the redemption which is in Christ Jesus; whom God displayed publicly as a propitiation in His blood through faith. This was to demonstrate His righteousness, because in the forbearance of God He passed over the sins previously committed; for the demonstration, I say, of His righteousness at the present time, so that He would be just and the justifier of the one who has faith in Jesus.
>
> — ROMANS 3:23-26

FEBRUARY 23

"Praise Him for his faithfulness and glory shining bright"

Even if we have lived horrendous lives full of trauma and trial, *someone* has gotten us to where we are right now! We have made it this far! That someone, of course, is Jesus Christ! He is so faithful.

Take time today to step back from the present circumstances of your life and allow the Holy Spirit to show you *His* perspective. You will see the faithfulness of God unfold in before unseen ways. Be grateful and thank Him. He has bestowed upon you the glory of His faithfulness. Praise Him for it!

> Why are you in despair, O my soul?
>   And why have you become disturbed within me?
>   Hope in God, for I shall again praise Him
>   For the help of His presence.

— PSALM 42:5

FEBRUARY 24

"Praise the Holy Spirit, the Father, and the Son"

It is good to praise the Lord. Praise involves our entire being and focuses our attention away from ourselves and onto a Kingdom perspective. Spend time today meditating on what it means for God to be your Father. Spend time today meditating on what it means to be led by the Spirit. Spend time today meditating on what sonship or daughtership with God means as you focus on *the* Son, Jesus Christ. As an act of praise, allow the truths revealed to you to permeate every area of your life!

> I and the Father are one.

— JOHN 10:30

FEBRUARY 25

"Praise unto Almighty God! The Lord of All is One!"

Father is God. Jesus is God. The Holy Spirit is God. Three in One. Talk about power! Sometimes we need Him as Father, and He is there. Sometimes we need Him as Brother, and He is there. Sometimes we need His comfort and guidance, and He is there. God is everything we need regardless of whether we realize it.

Think of the power available to the one who recognizes this truth, believes it, and infuses this truth into his or her life! Do that today! Infuse your life with the truth that God is absolutely everything you need.

Hear, O Israel! The Lord is our God, the Lord is one!

— DEUTERONOMY 6:4

But the one who joins himself to the Lord is one spirit with Him.

— 1 CORINTHIANS 6:17

FEBRUARY 26

"Lord, build in me the faith to go like Shadrach, Meshach, and Abednego"

Listen to the song "Servants Of The Most High God" from the album *We Are The Army.*

Lord, build in me the faith to go-
Like Shadrach, Meshach and Abednego!
And through the fire I will go
Like Shadrach, Meshach and Abednego!

What Satan means for evil
You will mean for good!
So fill me with Your holy fire
And with the one who stood beside them!

We are servants of the Most High God!
Servants of the Most High King!

Tho' the flames surround you
His love will abound to

Servants of the Most High God!
We are servants of the Most High God!

In God's Word we are told of three valiant men of faith named Shadrach, Meshach, and Abednego. In captivity, they were faced with the option of denying their faith to spare their lives or with choosing to live out their faith and be put to death. They held to their faith and were subsequently thrown into a fiery pit.

They must have known that life was not worth living when not lived in the reality of their identity as people of faith. Abundant life comes when we live according to our calling and our destiny, even if that life is cut short. Even if our lives our short, they can be overwhelmingly abundant and satisfied when we live each moment fully embracing our true identity in Christ.

Live well today. Walk as a son or daughter of the King!

Nebuchadnezzar responded and said to them, "Is it true, Shadrach, Meshach and Abed-nego, that you do not serve my gods or worship the golden image that I have set up? Now if you are ready, at the moment you hear the sound of the horn, flute, lyre, trigon, psaltery and bagpipe and all kinds of music, to fall down and worship the image that I have made, very well. But if you do not worship, you will immediately be cast into the midst of a furnace of blazing fire; and what god is there who can deliver you out of my hands?"

Shadrach, Meshach and Abed-nego replied to the king, "O Nebuchadnezzar, we do not need to give you an answer concerning this matter. If it be so, our God whom we serve is able to deliver us from the furnace of blazing fire; and He will deliver us out of your hand, O king."

— DANIEL 3:14-17

FEBRUARY 27

"And through the fire I will go like Shadrach, Meshach, and Abednego"

Those men went through a literal fire and God sustained them! In fact, He was *in the fire with them*! When we go through fiery trials in life, we must acknowledge that God is in those trials *with* us. We are never alone. We can say we are living victoriously when *the God of the universe* goes through our trials with us! Regardless of what we face, there is hope. Regardless of what we are called to endure, there is grace. Regardless of what we feel or don't feel, what we see or don't see, our God is *with* us!

Think on this today and *live well*! Live victoriously!

Then these men were tied up in their trousers, their coats, their caps and their other clothes, and were cast into the midst of the furnace of blazing fire. For this reason, because the king's command was urgent and the furnace had been made extremely hot, the flame of the fire slew those men who carried up Shadrach, Meshach and Abed-nego. But these three men, Shadrach, Meshach and Abed-nego, fell into the midst of the furnace of blazing fire still tied up.

Then Nebuchadnezzar the king was astounded and stood up in haste; he said to his high officials, "Was it not three men we cast bound into the midst of the fire?" They replied to the king, "Certainly, O king." He said, "Look! I see four men loosed and walking about in the midst of the fire without harm, and the appearance of the fourth is like a son of the gods!" Then Nebuchadnezzar came near to the door of the furnace of blazing fire; he responded and said, "Shadrach, Meshach and Abed-nego, come out, you servants of the Most High God, and come here!" Then Shadrach, Meshach and Abed-nego came out of the midst of the fire.

— DANIEL 3:21-26

FEBRUARY 28

"What Satan means for evil You will mean for good"

God wastes nothing if we bring it to Him. Evil? He turns to our good and His glory. Trials? He gives us grace to endure and a story of deliverance to tell. Wounds? He brings healing and leaves scars that testify to His greatness and love in our lives. I heard this quote recently: the pessimist may be right but the optimist enjoys the journey! The truth is that God does not waste a thing in the journey of life. We must simply practice honest, open, intimate confession and allow Him to bring about transformation in the process!

Put on the Kingdom point of view today and live life abundantly regardless of your circumstances. Live well today, Kingdom child!

> And we know that God causes all things to work together for good to those who love God, to those who are called according to His purpose.
>
> — ROMANS 8:28

FEBRUARY 29

"What Satan means for evil You will mean for good"

Spend time today focusing on your gratitude to God and others for all they have done to get you to where you are. If it helps, make a list of things God has done and give thanks accordingly. Tell others about what you experience afterward. Make a list of people who have been instrumental in your journey and consider calling or emailing or writing a short note to thank them for being used by God in your life!

> Oh give thanks to the Lord, call upon His name;
> Make known His deeds among the peoples.

— 1 CHRONICLES 16:8

MARCH

MARCH 1

"So, fill me with Your holy fire and with the One who stood beside them"

Why would we ever choose to fill our minds with thoughts contrary to what is good and right and beneficial? Often, especially during times of stress and duress, we allow the lies of the enemy to dictate our choices. Our true reality is that we have direct access to God and His mind and have been given the grace to choose wisely in *any* circumstance. The same God that went through the fire with Shadrach, Meshach, and Abednego is the same God that goes through the fire with us.

Fill your mind with thoughts that set you up to make good choices and do not be so quick to take the enemy's easy way out.

Finally, brethren, whatever is true, whatever is honorable, whatever is right, whatever is pure, whatever is lovely, whatever is of good repute, if there is any excellence and if anything worthy of praise, dwell on these things. The things you have learned and received and heard and seen in me, practice these things, and the God of peace will be with you.

— PHILIPPIANS 4:8-9

MARCH 2

"We are servants of the Most High God!"

We are servants of the Most High God called—as new creations—to be ministers of reconciliation. Whatever our gifts or personalities or occupation, the underlying reality is that each of us is called to help others become reconciled to God through faith in Christ Jesus. As servants, we are not here for our good pleasure or our own glory, but rather we are here for *His* good pleasure and *His* glory.

In all we say, do, or think today, let us remember we are servants of the Most High God. Let your attitude reflect your identity in Christ and preach your sermon—whether you ever speak a word or not!

But it is not this way among you, but whoever wishes to become great among you shall be your servant; and whoever wishes to be first among you shall be slave of all. For even the Son of Man did not come to be served, but to serve, and to give His life a ransom for many.

— MARK 10:43-45

MARCH 3

"We are servants of the Most High King!"

If we truly are servants of the Most High King—Jesus Christ—then let us put our faith in practice today. Sometimes the greatest sermons are not expressed with words, but rather by the acts of love we minister to others.

Today, ask the Holy Spirit to make you very aware of and sensitive to the needs around you. Open the door for another. Offer a drink of water to that thirsty soul. Help a hurried officemate with a task. Just be ready, as you start your day, to be servant of the Most High King in the most practical ways. Bathe all you say, think, or do in prayer and an attitude of love.

And whoever in the name of a disciple gives to one of these little ones even a cup of cold water to drink, truly I say to you, he shall not lose his reward.

— MATTHEW 10:42

MARCH 4

"Though the flames surround you"

The flames of affliction can often seem overwhelming. Just as when faced with a physical fire, we try and get as much distance between us and the flames as possible. In a spiritual sense, we try to do the same thing. We often take the easiest way out of a predicament, when the truth of the matter is, a

Kingdom perspective may show that our best outcome will be revealed as we take the journey *through* the flames of trial. When gold is heated, fire causes the impurities to rise to the surface. Once those impurities are revealed, the refiner scoops them away, leaving a purer metal.

Today, do not be so quick to get out of the fire. God has grace for you to endure. Allow the impurities to rise to the surface and quickly give them to the Lord to scoop away! You'll come out shining like gold!

> He will sit as a smelter and purifier of silver, and He will purify the sons of Levi and refine them like gold and silver, so that they may present to the Lord offerings in righteousness.
>
> — MALACHI 3:3

MARCH 5

"His love will abound to servants of the Most High God!"

God's love is like an endless sea whose shores and depths are unfathomable. Because we are His children—servants of the Most High God—we have direct and constant access to that love. To the degree that you have experienced His love, be prepared to extend that love in worship back to God. To the degree that His love has been lavished upon you, be prepared to lavish that love on those around you today. Love in thought.

Love in attitude. Love in action as you give your life in service to others. God will be magnified in the process.

> Whatever you do in word or deed, do all in the name of the Lord Jesus, giving thanks through Him to God the Father.

> — COLOSSIANS 3:17

MARCH 6

"Some trust in chariots"

Chariots, the horse-drawn battle tanks of ancient days, were dreaded by those unfortunate enough to be beset by them. For some, the chariot represented ultimate power, and whoever went to battle with the most chariots held the upper hand. The enemy wants us to believe his army of lies is invincible. When my mind is overrun by his onslaught of lies, I must place my faith in the strength of the Lord. When we place our trust in our own mental capacity, physical strength, talents, or anything other than the Lord, we fall in defeat and give in to temptation. Let us place our trust and find our strength in the truth of God's Word. God's Word prevails over the vast army of the enemy's lies.

Today, let us put our faith and trust in the Lord and thereby defeat the lies of the enemy that pursue us like an army of chariots. Put him down with the weapons of your warfare!

> For though we walk in the flesh, we do not war according to the flesh, for the weapons of our warfare are not of the flesh, but divinely powerful for the destruction of fortresses. We

are destroying speculations and every lofty thing raised up against the knowledge of God, and we are taking every thought captive to the obedience of Christ.

— 2 CORINTHIANS 10:3-5

MARCH 7

"Some trust in horses"

Sometimes we allow our spiritual maturity to give way to human logic in unhealthy ways. When we have been walking with the Lord many years and become confident in our ability to discern the lies of the enemy from the truth of God, we can mistakenly think we had something to do with that maturity. Then, we begin to walk in our own strength. Regardless of how mature I may grow in the Lord, it is my humble heart and attitude that ensure the process of maturity continues. I may have been granted great discernment, but who is the One who *truly* gives that discernment to me? Of course it is the Lord.

Today, let us simply remind ourselves not to trust in our own strength but bolster our faith by relying on God's strength to get us through.

My flesh and my heart may fail,
But God is the strength of my heart and my portion forever.

— PSALM 73:26

MARCH 8

"Some trust in chariots but I will trust in the Lord"

When we place our hope in things, or people, or jobs, or talents we set ourselves up for failure. Our *only* hope is in our relationship with Jesus Christ. When things break or fall into disrepair, Jesus is still there. When people betray us or leave or die, Jesus is still there. When work dries up and finances are slim, Jesus is still there. When our talents let us down, or someone more talented comes along, Jesus is still there.

Where is your trust today? Is it built on Solid Ground or sinking sand? Set yourself up for victory today by placing your trust in Jesus.

> Why are you in despair, O my soul?
>> And why are you disturbed within me?
>> Hope in God, for I shall again praise Him,
>> The help of my countenance and my God.

— PSALM 43:5

MARCH 9

"Hallelujah! Halle-Hallelujah!"

Certain words have certain anointings. The word *hallelujah*, for instance, resounds with joy and seems to bolster the heart . This word from the Greek language means "praise the Lord," but its basis is from the Hebrew word *halal* which means "to boast in" or "to make a fool of oneself." When your favorite team scores a touchdown, how do you respond? Crazy right? Jesus scored eternal victory for you and I. The word *hallelujah* is appropriate when we worship the Lord.

To the degree that you have been redeemed, boast in the Lord today and use *hallelujah* as needed! And remember, if you are unashamed to boast in your favorite team, why would you ever cower from boasting in your Redeemer? Just a thought.

Praise the Lord! [Hallelujah!]
Oh give thanks to the Lord, for He is good;
For His lovingkindness is everlasting.

— PSALM 106:1

MARCH 10

"I will trust upon the Lord"

Life is precarious at times. Sometimes, we feel like we are walking on a financial ledge and one misstep will spell disaster. Sometimes, we feel overwhelmed emotionally, and it seems we teeter between sanity and stability. When we are on one of the precipices of life, it is wise to have someone hold our hand and help us maintain balance. There is only One who can truly *always* be there.

Let us spend time today seeing life from the King's perspective and allowing Him to hold our hand as we traverse the steep ledges of life. He will maintain us. He will sustain us. He will always be there. Jesus is faithful. Take advantage of that reality today.

The Lord is my rock and my fortress and my deliverer;

    My God, my rock, in whom I take refuge,

    My shield and the horn of my salvation, my stronghold
and my refuge;

    My savior, You save me from violence.

    I call upon the Lord, who is worthy to be praised,

    And I am saved from my enemies.

— 2 SAMUEL 22:2-4

MARCH 11

"And I sing glory, glory!"

Glory is simply the weight of God's presence. Sometimes the weight of His presence is so palpable that we get consumed emotionally—perhaps while in intensely deep and personal times of worship. Sometimes the weight of God's presence is almost unnoticeable—when we feel led to perform some seemingly minor service for another and feel a tinge of satisfaction. God's glory is full of joy and full of wonder, and yet we often miss His glory when we do not remind ourselves that He constantly surrounds us with His presence.

Take time today to revel in God's glory. Do not be surprised to see it in the mundane. God's glory is not dependent upon our emotional state. He is with us. And when we are with Him, so is His glory.

The heavens are telling of the glory of God;

    And their expanse is declaring the work of His hands.

— PSALM 19:1

MARCH 12

"I will trust upon the Lord"

Today, let's practice trusting the Lord in small ways and see what He reveals in the process. As you prepare for the day, ask Him to show you what to wear. As you drive to work or run errands, allow Him to arrange your schedule. When you meet someone, ask the Lord to reveal a way you can meet a need in that person's life. If you listen to the radio or watch TV, ask the Lord to guide your listening and viewing. These may seem like trivial exercises, but trust is built as we spend time talking with someone. Believing you can hear His voice is, in itself, an act of trust.

Step out today and trust that you *can* hear the voice of your Shepherd, and enjoy the building of that trust.

> But let all who take refuge in You be glad,
> Let them ever sing for joy;
> And may You shelter them,
> That those who love Your name may exult in You.

> — PSALM 5:11

MARCH 13

"Some boast in chariots"

When we are confident in something—like our team's ability to win or our physical or mental prowess—we tend to boast about those things. But what happens when our unbeatable team falls to defeat, or we grow physically weak or mentally fragile? We do not boast then, do we? I have good news for us! Even when things fall apart around us, and even when we grow physically weak or are challenged in some other way, our God is faithful! He is a rock that cannot be shaken and will not be moved, and He is a God who is jealous for His children! That means we can *always* boast in our God!

Even if you do not *feel* like boasting in Him today, do it any way and allow your faith to break through the lies of the enemy and into the truth of who and whose you are!

> I have set the Lord continually before me;
>> Because He is at my right hand, I will not be shaken.

> — PSALM 16:8

MARCH 14

"Some boast in horses"

A horse is a mighty creature, full of muscle and brute strength. Back in the days when horses were the used in battle, it was common practice to weaken a cavalry's power by taking the horses out of commission. If a foot soldier could get in a position near the rear of the animal, he could use his sword to slice the hamstring of the beast and render the animal of no more use to its rider. When we rely on our own strength, we often feel invincible — until the circumstances of life or the lies of the enemy hamstring our minds.

Let us not boast in anything but our Savior today. By doing so, we effectively render our minds prepared for victory by covering them with the helmet of salvation. Put on faith today and boast in the power of your God, and hamstring the lies of the enemy in the process.

> Therefore, take up the full armor of God, so that you will be able to resist in the evil day, and having done everything, to stand firm. Stand firm therefore, having girded your loins with truth, and having put on the breastplate of righteousness, and having shod your feet with the preparation of the gospel of peace; in addition to all, taking up the shield of faith with which you will be able to extinguish all the flaming arrows of the evil one. And take the helmet of salvation, and the sword of the Spirit, which is the word of God.
>
> — EPHESIANS 6:13-17

MARCH 15

"Some boast in chariots but I will boast in the Lord"

We tend to boast in that in which we place our trust. Some people boast about their jobs and the money they make. Some people boast about their abilities or athletic prowess. Some people boast in their power. Some people boast in their mental capacity and creativity. While there is nothing inherently wrong with any of those things, it is foolish for us to place our hope and trust in any of them. Jobs can be lost. Money can wither away. Abilities can lessen with age or circumstance. Power is fleeting. Intellect and creativity can be lost. One thing —one Person—never changes. And He holds all things together, having spoken them into existence in the first place.

Let us remember this today and boast in the God who made all things possible. Let us use the things He has given us to glorify and boast in *His* creativity and power and love!

For in Him we live and move and exist, as even some of your own poets have said, "For we also are His children."

— ACTS 17:28

MARCH 16

"The lion comes but to steal and destroy"

The enemy of God — Satan — is a liar. His only power is that of deception. He comes to deceive our minds into thinking we are not called to be sons and daughters of God. If he can pervert our concept of identity, he can control our life. If he can control the way we think of ourselves, he will most assuredly lead us to destruction. Make no bones about it, he lives and breathes to bring us down. But the Good News is that we are victorious over him as new creations in Christ! Reality is that this lion is all roar and no bite!

Today, stop listening to the roar of his deception concerning who you are and send him on his way, tail tucked between his legs, by proclaiming the truth of who and of whose you are.

The thief comes only to steal and kill and destroy; I came that they may have life, and have it abundantly.

— JOHN 10:10

"But I have the heart of the Shepherd boy"

As we think of ourselves in our heart, so we will be. When we put garbage in our minds, we get garbage out. When we plant weeds, we sow weeds. It is of paramount importance that we put off the lies of the enemy and put on the truth of who God says we are. Just as the shepherd boy, David, was not cowed at the thought of protecting his father's flocks from the bear and the lion, we are not to be cowed at the lies of the enemy. David simply *believed* he was the caregiver and protector of those flocks, and as he believed, so he acted!

As we recognize the enemy's lies and call them what they are, we must pick up the slings of our faith, put in the rock of the truth, and cast it at the lions and bears surrounding us. If God calls you a new creation, simply believe you are a new creation and act like a new creation. As we think we are sons and daughters of God, our attitudes follow. As our attitudes change, our behavior follows suit.

Remember, you are not defined by your past, by your present, nor by the things that tempt you. Only One gets to define you. Be his mighty son or daughter of faith today and put the enemy to flight in your own life. Rejoice at the victory our God has afforded you!

Then Saul said to David, "You are not able to go against this Philistine to fight with him; for you are but a youth while he has been a warrior from his youth." But David said to Saul, "Your servant was tending his father's sheep. When a lion or a bear came and took a lamb from the flock, I went out after him and attacked him, and rescued it from his mouth; and when he rose up against me, I seized him by his beard and struck him and killed him. Your servant has killed both the lion and the bear; and this uncircumcised Philistine will be like one of them, since he has taunted the armies of the living God." And David said, "The Lord who delivered me from the paw of the lion and from the paw of the bear, He will deliver me from the hand of this Philistine." And Saul said to David, "Go, and may the Lord be with you."

— 1 SAMUEL 17:33-37

MARCH 18

"In my sling is the Rock of the Ages"

When David was a young boy and his father taught him to wield a sling, I am sure he was not always able to hit the target. Did that mean he should stop trying? Of course not. Falling does not equal failure. Failure only occurs when we decide to just not get back up. When responding to the fiery darts of the enemy's lies, we must believe that God has given us the power and tools necessary to defeat those lies. First, we must believe we are overcomers because of our victory in Christ. Then we must practice hitting the target by constantly putting on the truth.

Like a sling, put your faith into practice. Fill that sling with the Rock of Jesus Christ and His Word. Cast the Word—the name of Jesus—at the lies and watch them fall! How long should we cast those stones of truth at the lies of the enemy? As long as necessary!

Do some target practice today and be who your God says you are!

And they overcame him because of the blood of the Lamb and because of the word of their testimony, and they did not love their life even when faced with death.

— REVELATION 12:11

MARCH 19

"In my mouth is the song of the King"

There is something to be said about singing a song in the face of hard times. In our own nation's history, many songs were born on the backs of slaves laboring in the fields of oppression. The songs helped get them through the long, harsh days of pain and suffering. When children are young and fearful of the night, what does a mother or father do almost instinctively at their bedside? They sing to that child and watch the fear melt into peaceful slumber. Singing requires our entire being, engaging our body, our will, our thoughts, our senses, and our emotions into one laser-focused place of power. When our songs are focused on God or the needs of others, the enemy has no place in which to set one of his fiery lies.

Today, be ready to take every thought captive when the enemy attacks. Consider the power of a song of praise to your King. Your soul will be lifted, the enemy placed under your feet where he belongs and, above all else, God will be glorified!

My heart overflows with a good theme;

I address my verses to the King;
My tongue is the pen of a ready writer.

— PSALM 45:1

MARCH 20

"And my feet will run to the roar of the beast"

Often, when face with a fearful situation or conflict, we run the opposite direction and try to avoid facing the object of that fear. If we ever hope to be free, we must get to the place of honest confession, and part of honest confession is admitting our fear. But we must be willing to take that confession one step further, and *face* that fear. Otherwise, it will always hold power over us. Do you have conflict with another? Talk with them. Are you afraid to fail? You will never succeed if you don't take that first step. David did not wait for Goliath to come to Him — he went out and faced him, and won. Jesus did not wait for the cross to come to Him — he went to the cross, and won.

Face your fears today and see them from God's perspective. In this place of vision, we see that which we fear for what it truly is: an opportunity to know a deeper place in the power of God's grace.

Be of sober spirit, be on the alert. Your adversary, the devil, prowls around like a roaring lion, seeking someone to devour. But resist him, firm in your faith, knowing that the same experiences of suffering are being accomplished by your brethren who are in the world. After you have suffered for a little while, the God of all grace, who called you to His eternal glory in Christ, will Himself perfect, confirm, strengthen and establish you.

— 1 PETER 5:8-10

MARCH 21

"As I cry to the north, south, west, and east"

What areas of your life do you still feel defeated in? Did Jesus die to free us from just part of our bondage or to free us from all of the things that bind us? As I have walked with Jesus I have discovered that there are always new places of freedom He desires to take me to—but I never get there if I am fearful or if I believe His grace is not sufficient. Just as I do not want to put God in a box and thereby limit what He can do in my life, I do not want to put myself in a box and thereby limit what I can do in my life! My desire is that the Lord take back all of the stolen ground of my life and extend my boundaries— to the north, south, east, and west.

Cry out to the Lord today, believe Him for the best in your life, and be prepared to take back whatever stolen ground He reveals.

Oh give thanks to the Lord, for He is good,
For His lovingkindness is everlasting.
Let the redeemed of the Lord say so,
Whom He has redeemed from the hand of the adversary

And gathered from the lands,
From the east and from the west,
From the north and from the south.

— PSALM 107:1-3

~

MARCH 22

"Give up!"

We have power and authority over the enemy and his lies. You and I, as new creations in Christ, have only to declare the truth in order to shine the light of Jesus on the dark and barren places of our lives. We can speak the truth of Jesus to our own soul and watch the despair melt away into hope. We can speak the truth of Jesus to the things in our lives that *used* to define us and walk in the freedom of our *true* identity in Christ. We can speak life to the dead places in our lives by calling ourselves what our Father calls us.

Spend time today be very intentional about what you say and think about yourself. Do not allow past definitions to define you. Allow only Father to define you. Speak to the north, south, east, and west of your memory—of your life— and flood those places with truth, commanding the lies to "give up" to the truth of who Jesus says you are!

Death and life are in the power of the tongue,
And those who love it will eat its fruit.

— PROVERBS 18:21

MARCH 23

"Run to the roar!"

Satan goes around like a roaring lion, trying to frighten us into believing his lies about who we are. If he can do that, he can keep us from realizing our full destiny in Christ. Satan's only power is in his deception. In effect, he is merely a toothless lion who *only* has a roar but no bite! We put him under our feet where he belongs when we run *to* the roar by declaring the truth of God's Word. We have nothing to fear. God has not given us a spirit of fear, but he *has* given us a spirit of power.

Walk in the power of who Father says you are today. Run *to* the roar and watch the enemy flee.

> Be of sober spirit, be on the alert. Your adversary, the devil, prowls around like a roaring lion, seeking someone to devour. But resist him, firm in your faith.
>
> — 1 PETER 5:8-9B

MARCH 24

"Give up!"

There is one thing a believer can give up hope about. We can give up the hope of changing our past! It cannot be done! What do we do with our past? We offer it to the Lord in broken honesty and allow Him to use it as He will—for our own good and for His glory. When we own our past and are freed from its shame by giving it openly and honestly to Jesus, the past no longer has power over us. Just as we speak truth to the enemy and put him under our feet, we speak to our own souls and give up trying to change something that cannot be changed. The beauty of that is in *knowing* God will use even our failure for our good and His glory.

Why waste your time wishing you could change your past? Stop dragging it around with you. Let it go and walk into your destiny and identity in Christ.

> Brethren, I do not regard myself as having laid hold of it yet; but one thing I do: forgetting what lies behind and reaching forward to what lies ahead, I press on toward the goal for the prize of the upward call of God in Christ Jesus.

> — PHILIPPIANS 3:13-14

MARCH 25

"Run to the fight!"

Most of us do not like conflict, but without conflict, the enemy will continue to win the battles for our thoughts. We must recognize that we are in a fight for survival and that *the* battleground is our mind! As new creations, we have been given a vast arsenal of the truth with which to defeat the enemy. Why waste time cowering in fear of what might be, when we can run *to* the battle and engage the enemy with the truth of who God says we are? Here's the truth: we *win*!

Today, let us keep our eyes fixed on Jesus and put on the whole armor of God. Then, let us be quick to put the enemy down whenever he raises his ugly, lying head. You are victorious!

> Finally, be strong in the Lord and in the strength of His might. Put on the full armor of God, so that you will be able to stand firm against the schemes of the devil. For our struggle is not against flesh and blood, but against the rulers, against the powers, against the world forces of this darkness, against the spiritual forces of wickedness in the heavenly places. Therefore, take up the full armor of God, so that you will be able to resist in the evil day, and having done everything, to stand firm. Stand firm therefore, having girded your loins with truth, and having put on the breastplate of righteousness, and having shod your feet with the preparation of the Gospel of Peace; in addition to all, taking up the shield of faith with which you will be able to extinguish all the flaming arrows of the evil one. And take the helmet of salvation, and the sword of the Spirit, which is the word of God.

> — EPHESIANS 6:10-17

MARCH 26

"Give up!"

Let us focus today on going after ground the enemy has stolen from us. What areas of your life do you still feel weak or defeated in? Let those areas be the focus of your warfare today. When a thought comes up that causes you to feel shame, sorrow, or regret over some past failure or event, ask the Holy

Spirit to allow you to see what *He* sees. Put on His truth and believe it as the greater reality. We are citizens of the Kingdom of God, and we must view our lives as such.

Today, speak the truth to the shame and walk into the purity of your redemption. Tell the sorrow that God has replaced it with joy. Tell the regret to give up and surrender to the restoration of Jesus Christ in your life. Walk as one who knows they are redeemed, and command the lies of the enemy to give up to the truth of Jesus Christ.

> For though we walk in the flesh, we do not war according to the flesh, for the weapons of our warfare are not of the flesh, but divinely powerful for the destruction of fortresses. We are destroying speculations and every lofty thing raised up against the knowledge of God, and we are taking every thought captive to the obedience of Christ, and we are ready to punish all disobedience, whenever your obedience is complete.
>
> — 2 CORINTHIANS 10:3-6

MARCH 27

"Shout a song of victory!"

Shouting does a soul good! How do you feel when your team just scored that come-from-behind touchdown to win the game? You shout out loud! It is cleansing, and it is joyful, and it is exhilarating and life-affirming all at once! Imagine shouting like that to and for the Lord Jesus Christ who has secured your eternity! That's bigger than any touchdown! Your salvation is the major event of your life! With salvation comes a brand new identity and a joyful journey, with a very definite and holy destiny ordained of and by God *just for you*! We have reason to shout a song of victory!

Find time—whether in the car to work or some secluded place where you can let it all out—and sing and shout your victorious nature back to God! It'll do you good!

O clap your hands, all peoples;
　　Shout to God with the voice of joy.

　　　　　　　　　　　　　　　　　— PSALM 47:1

MARCH 28

"Bless the God of might!"

To bless someone is to bestow worth on that individual. The act of blessing also does something for the one who gives the blessing. When we acknowledge the worth of God in our lives, we effectively put the enemy and his lies to flight—they cannot stand under the weight of God's truth. In the same instant that we bless God, we receive the blessing of humility. As we intentionally bless Him, the life born of our relationship with Him floods back on our own being.

Bless His name today, and give Him the glory due His name. Thank Him for His many benefits—and find your own soul blessed in the process.

Bless the Lord, O my soul,

And all that is within me, bless His holy name.

Bless the Lord, O my soul,

And forget none of His benefits.

— PSALM 103:1-2

MARCH 29

"Give up! Oh! Give up!"

Let today be a day where you actively command the enemy to give up. Speak to the lies when they become apparent to you. Replace them with the truth of who Father says you are. Do not be swayed by feelings, but rather put on the truth and put the enemy under your feet where he belongs. Then, watch feelings of triumph and security and righteousness and life flood your entire being. Do not waste time thinking of yourself in any terms other than what your Father says about you. He wants only your best. Tell any contrary thought they might as well give up to the truth! Walk in victory today. You *are* a victor!

> "For I know the plans that I have for you," declares the Lord, "plans for welfare and not for calamity to give you a future and a hope. Then you will call upon Me and come and pray to Me, and I will listen to you. You will seek Me and find Me when you search for Me with all your heart."

— JEREMIAH 29:11-13

MARCH 30

"North, give up!"

When we begin taking back ground the enemy has stolen, we often face the cold harshness of past failures. But I have great news—God forgives! If you have not already done so, ask the Lord to forgive you of past failures. Then, believe He has done so, receive that forgiveness, and go on! If you have received His forgiveness but still battle feelings of not being forgiven, have you forgiven *yourself*? Your standards are not higher than God's, so forgive yourself and go on. In doing so, you will crush the cold darkness of your past, and your heart will be armed with the thoughts of being made clean and whole by the blood of Jesus!

> In Him we have redemption through His blood, the forgiveness of our trespasses, according to the riches of His grace which He lavished on us.
>
> — EPHESIANS 1:7-8

MARCH 31

"South, give up!"

What are the deepest places of your heart where you have not allowed the grace and light of God to shine in a while? Are your weary in any area of your soul? Are you worn out from pouring out your heart and life for others? Would it be good to just lay down and rest in your soul? We can do that right now. Be honest about your own needs today, and confess to the Lord your desire and need for rest. Once you do that, be prepared to obey Him and rest! Lay down your agenda today and prioritize your life accordingly. Do not be afraid to say no to people. Fellowship with God and simply pour out your personal need for refreshment on Him. He will meet you there.

Come to Me, all who are weary and heavy-laden, and I will give you rest. Take My yoke upon you and learn from Me, for I am gentle and humble in heart, and you will find rest for your souls. For My yoke is easy and My burden is light.

— MATTHEW 11:28-30

APRIL

APRIL 1

"East, give up!"

Sometimes, life can take us to places where we feel like we are up against a wall. Difficult decisions can bring us to the brink of life and death. God's Word tells us that we can find wisdom by searching the heart of God. When we are faced with difficult decisions, it is wise to get to the place where we can see what Father sees. Real wisdom is simply seeing life from God's perspective. And even when our feeble human eyes seem clouded by all the surrounding factors, we can hear His voice, we can read His word, and we can follow the leadership of the Holy Spirit.

Speak to the undecided areas of your life with the wisdom of God. Seek Him today and be led from His point of view.

Your word is a lamp to my feet
And a light to my path.

— PSALM 119:105

APRIL 2

"West, give up!"

When I think of the western USA, I think of deserts and barrenness. Life will take us through times of barrenness and we will go through times of spiritual dryness. Not to worry. Even in the barren and dry places of life, our God will be a stream in our midst, abundantly supplying our needs and giving us grace to endure the barren and dry times.

Today, command the dry and barren places to give up to God's presence and be filled with Living Water. Walk in faith regardless of how dry you feel. Walk in hope regardless of how barren the enemy wants you to believe your life is. You are not alone, and the Lord will meet every need. Trust Him.

Do not call to mind the former things,
　　Or ponder things of the past.
　　Behold, I will do something new,
　　Now it will spring forth;
　　Will you not be aware of it?
　　I will even make a roadway in the wilderness,
　　Rivers in the desert.

— ISAIAH 43:18-19

APRIL 3

"You're gonna give up!"

There is no way around it. In Christ—as a new creation—you have been given the heart of a giant killer. Rather than cowering at the whims of the enemy today, why not walk as one who has already won the battle? Rather than being defeated by one of his subtle lies before you step out of the door, why not walk as one who knows they have been redeemed regardless of what the enemy says. Speak to your own soul and remind yourself of who you are, and remind yourself of *whose* you are. Be God's man or woman. Be nothing less than who *He* says you are!

> For this reason I also suffer these things, but I am not ashamed; for I know whom I have believed and I am convinced that He is able to guard what I have entrusted to Him until that day.
>
> — 1 TIMOTHY 1:12

APRIL 4

"Everything in my life I give up to You"

Listen to the song "Not Even Death" from the album *We Are The Army*.

87

Ev'ry thing in my life I give up to You –
Many doubts and many fears and many lies!
Ev'ry burden I may bear, ev'ry sorrow ev'ry care
I release with ev'ry truth I realize!

Not even death – Not even life –
Can separate Your love from me
You gave your life!

Not mountains high! Not valleys low –
Can keep me from Your love I know!
Not Satan's angels! Not Satan's lies –
Nor Satan's power ever realize!

That nothing present and nothing past
Nor things to come – these things won't last!
Not even death – Not even life –
Can separate Your love from my life!

All the clouds and darkest nights seem to vanish from my sight,
Ev'ry ripple seems to calm as You draw near!
As temptations come my way I will be your willing clay!
Take this vessel, Lord, and made it crystal clear!

When we come to the Lord for salvation, He completely cleanses us from all our sin. Yet, as we live our lives *after* the point of salvation, we often fall back into old ways of thinking that are completely contrary to our forgiven, redeemed nature. Such thinking reduces us to our own strength and makes us susceptible to the lies of the enemy. Make a habit of daily cleansing your soul—confessing wrong thoughts and attitudes in honesty to the Lord—and watch the old life fade from view. Such emptying of our souls is healthy for every aspect of our life. As you walk clean before the Lord, watch the power of your true identity in Christ burst forth in confidence.

Today, just be who He says you are!

For with the heart a person believes, resulting in righteousness, and with the mouth he confesses, resulting in salvation.

— ROMANS 10:10

~

APRIL 5

"Many doubts and many fears and many lies"

Are there any areas of doubt in your life today? Are there any areas of fear? It stands to reason that you will be able to link those doubts and fears directly to some lie of the enemy. This is a good place to walk in faith and trust of who God is and in the confidence of who He says you are. In the place of doubt, put on the Word of God. In the place of fear, put on the Word of God. In the place of lies, put on the Word of God. The Word of God has a way of leading us out of fear and doubt and into life-giving relationship with our Redeemer God. Walk in faith today.

Trust in the Lord with all your heart

And do not lean on your own understanding.
In all your ways acknowledge Him,
And He will make your paths straight.
Do not be wise in your own eyes;
Fear the Lord and turn away from evil.
It will be healing to your body
And refreshment to your bones.

— PROVERBS 3:5-8

APRIL 6

"Every burden I may bear"

God's Word tells us He will not allow us to be tempted beyond what we can bear. Yet we often feel so overwhelmed by our temptations that we can hardly function. Our minds are constantly being bombarded by the lies of the enemy. This bombardment tends to cause us to draw within ourselves and get us self-focused — right where the enemy wants us.

Let us practice taking our eyes off of our selves today by focusing on the needs of others. If you are tempted to give up hope, look to encourage a hopeless person. If you are tempted to feel rejected, look to make a rejected person feel accepted. You get the idea. Turn the tables on the lies of the enemy, and use the lies as fuel for righteous choices and attitudes. You will glorify God in the process and make a channel for God's grace directly to your own need.

No temptation has overtaken you but such as is common to man; and God is faithful, who will not allow you to be tempted beyond what you are able, but with the temptation will provide the way of escape also, so that you will be able to endure it.

— 1 CORINTHIANS 10:13

Bear one another's burdens, and thereby fulfill the law of Christ.

— GALATIANS 6:2

APRIL 7

"Every sorrow"

Life is full of sorrow. That is simple reality due to sin. Sin ushered in death and destruction and despair and all that goes with it—but the great news is that we have a God who redeemed us from the curse of sin. As new creations—as Kingdom Seekers—we have been given access to a new perspective. Yes, we endure sorrow, but we now approach it from the King's point of view rather than our own. In the process, we discover more of who He is and more of who we are, and our sorrow is met by His comforting arms and grace. We are healed and He is glorified.

See today's disappointments from the King's point of view and walk in victory. Be prepared to minister comfort to sorrowing souls you may encounter through the day.

The Spirit of the Lord God is upon me,
  Because the Lord has anointed me
  To bring good news to the afflicted;
  He has sent me to bind up the brokenhearted,
  To proclaim liberty to captives
  And freedom to prisoners;
  To proclaim the favorable year of the Lord
  And the day of vengeance of our God;
  To comfort all who mourn.

— ISAIAH 61:1-2

APRIL 8

"Every care I release with every truth I realize"

Don't you love lightbulb moments? You know, the moment when you realize you have believed a lie about yourself and God reveals the truth and your entire being is lifted to a whole new plane of freedom? Far too often, we allow ourselves to be defined by the things that tempt us. Far too often, we allow ourselves to be defined by our past failures. Far too often, we allow ourselves to be defined by other people. Far too often, we allow ourselves to be defined by a feeling. Far too often, we allow ourselves to be defined by what we do for a living. There is only One who gets to define us — our Creator.

Spend time today peeling away the layers of those other things you have allowed to define you. Put those things off, and put on the truth of who Father says you are. Release yourself to be who God says you are, and watch a new attitude invade your mind and being. That is the power of freedom in Christ.

Cast your burden upon the Lord and He will sustain you;
He will never allow the righteous to be shaken.

— PSALM 55:22

APRIL 9

"Not even death"

What can truly separate us from the love of God? Can the words people say about us separate us from Him? Can the busyness of life truly ever separate us from His presence? Can the sorrows or cares of life separate us from Him? Can the rejection we feel at the hands of others separate us from His love? Can death separate us from Him? No! No! No! No! No! If we are new creations, *nothing* can separate us from His presence and love! We are in a covenant with God that He will not break! That truth alone should send shockwaves of freedom through our entire being! Not even *death* can separate us from Him!

Think about this truth today, and let His presence and love sustain you through the harshness life can bring.

Who will separate us from the love of Christ? Will tribulation, or distress, or persecution, or famine, or nakedness, or peril, or sword? Just as it is written, "For your sake we are being put to death all day long; we were considered as sheep to be slaughtered." But in all these things we overwhelmingly conquer through Him who loved us.

— ROMANS 8:35-37

"Not even life can separate Your love from me"

Sometimes we get so caught up in the busyness of life that we lose track of our relationships with family and friends. We also lose track of our relationship with the Lord. For relationship to truly serve its purpose—to nurture and bring forth life—that relationship must be cared for. A husband should take the time to connect to his wife or that relationship will suffer. A parent must take the time to connect with their children in order for that relationship to thrive. The good news is that Father God will not cut us off from Himself. It is we who cut ourselves off from Him.

Let us not allow the busyness of life to cause our relationship with Father to suffer. In going about your day, allow the Holy Spirit to remind you to interact with Father. You will receive life in the process. As you receive life from Father, release that same life relationally to family and friends. You will bless others and receive blessing in the process.

For I am convinced that neither death, nor life, nor angels, nor principalities, nor things present, nor things to come, nor powers, nor height, nor depth, nor any other created thing, will be able to separate us from the love of God, which is in Christ Jesus our Lord.

— ROMANS 8:38-39

"You gave Your life"

Jesus gave His life to gain relationship with us. There is an element of life that requires death. True love is not defined by a feeling, sexual or otherwise. True love is defined by the act of laying down one's life. When we lay down our life for another, what is the end result? The one we lay down our life for *lives*. The laying down of life is the ultimate act of love. Not sex. Just as Christ laid down His life for us and gave us new life, we are to lay down our lives and lead others to life in the process. Husbands lay down their lives for their wives. Mothers lay down their lives for their children. Policemen lay down their lives for our protection. Fireman lay down their lives for our safety. How do you feel after you have sacrificed for another? Satisfaction and freedom and *life* floods your entire being. Death always gives way to life. Always. Even physical death gives way to eternal life.

Think on these things today.

But when this perishable will have put on the imperishable, and this mortal will have put on immortality, then will come about the saying that is written, "Death is swallowed up in victory. O Death, where is your victory? O Death, where is your sting?"

— 1 CORINTHIANS 15:54-55

"Not mountains high"

Mountains can seem insurmountable—until you climb one! Before modern convenience and innovation, mankind had to go around or tediously scale a mountain to get to the other side. With modern technological advances, we can tunnel through a mountain or we can fly over it. But the beauty of the mountain is best seen by going through the canyons and over the peaks and into the valleys. The view from the top is amazing, but the green life is found in the low places. The Lord wants us to enjoy the journey of life—even in the low places. We should take a clue from nature and realize that the lush places in our journeys are where life thrives. It is good to see from the mountaintop, but life is truly enjoyed and lived fully in the valleys.

Let us not be so quick to try and tunnel our way through or to avoid the mountains altogether. Let us learn to enjoy the journey and see each and every aspect of our travels in life from the King's perspective. He is certainly on the mountaintops, but He is with us through the valleys as well!

Where can I go from Your Spirit?
Or where can I flee from Your presence?
If I ascend to heaven, You are there;
If I make my bed in Sheol, behold, You are there.
If I take the wings of the dawn,
If I dwell in the remotest part of the sea,
Even there Your hand will lead me,

And Your right hand will lay hold of me.

— PSALM 139:7-10

APRIL 13

"Not valleys low can keep me from Your love, I know"

It really does not matter how low our lives may seem. Our God is still able to reach into the lowest places we find ourselves and rescue us! His love is relentless. His love knows no bounds. His love far exceeds our human capacity to fully understand in this life. The amazing reality we live is that we get to spend this life receiving the lavish love of our God, then turn around and pour out that love to those around us!

Do not fear the valleys of life. See them as places where the love of God flows deeply and faithfully. Just as physical water always flows downward, the love of our God will flow down into the low places of our lives and sustain us. Be lifted up today by that love.

And hope does not disappoint, because the love of God has been poured out within our hearts through the Holy Spirit who was given to us. For while we were still helpless, at the right time Christ died for the ungodly.

— ROMANS 5:5-6

APRIL 14

"Not Satan's angels"

The enemy of God — Satan — is very real. His demons — his minions — are very real. But unlike God, they are not omnipresent. Their only true power is that of deception. Once we realize this, we must realize as well that we have the true power over them. In Christ we have the power to speak forth the name of Jesus and watch the enemy flee. In Christ we have the power to speak forth the truth and put down the lies. As new creations, we have been given the mind of Christ!

Let us practice who we are today by utilizing the very power granted to us by virtue of the blood of Jesus. When the lies come, put them down with the truth. When the enemy torments, put him away by proclaiming the name of Jesus!

> For who has known the mind of the Lord, that he will instruct him? But we have the mind of Christ.
>
> — 1 CORINTHIANS 2:16

APRIL 15

"Not Satan's lies"

What can separate us from the love of God? Distance? No, he is anywhere we are. Circumstances? No, he will use every circumstance for our good and His glory. The lies of the enemy? Only if we choose to believe them and walk in them! Satan is a liar who desires to get us so confused about our true identity that we never walk in or operate under the power granted to us by our place *in* Jesus!

Live, think, act, and breathe like one who is a joint-heir with Christ, believing that everything available to Jesus is available to us! Be the new creation you are called to be and walk boldly in that truth today!

> The Spirit Himself testifies with our spirit that we are children of God, and if children, heirs also, heirs of God and fellow heirs with Christ, if indeed we suffer with Him so that we may also be glorified with Him.
>
> — ROMANS 8:16-17

APRIL 16

"Nor Satan's power ever realize"

We have already established that Satan's only real power is deception. To overcome that deception we must put on the truth, even if we feel alone in life. King David's men once turned on him, threatening to kill him. David encouraged himself in the Lord. King Saul was once beset by evil spirits, and David played his harp—worshiped—and the enemy had to flee.

Today, let us practice the power God has granted us as new creations. When the enemy comes, encourage yourself in the Lord. When the enemy assails, worship the Lord right where you are. The enemy *will* flee, you will be strengthened in your soul, and God will receive all the glory!

> So it came about whenever the evil spirit from God came to Saul, David would take the harp and play it with his hand; and Saul would be refreshed and be well, and the evil spirit would depart from him.

> — 1 SAMUEL 16:23

~

APRIL 17

"That nothing present"

Sometimes we are overwhelmed with life by virtue of the sheer wall of circumstances that demands our attention. When all we can see is hard times, despair, or rejection, it is difficult to see what God is really up to. It is of utmost importance that we learn to see life, and to live life, from God's point of view rather than our own. When we are able to see even a small glimpse of our circumstances from God's perspective, those circumstances don't seem so insurmountable as they once did, and their power over our minds is drastically subdued.

Let us subdue the enemy today by getting to God's point of view concerning life's circumstances. Trust the Holy Spirit to guide you there.

> For I am convinced that neither death, nor life, nor angels, nor principalities, nor things present, nor things to come, nor

powers, nor height, nor depth, nor any other created thing, will be able to separate us from the love of God, which is in Christ Jesus our Lord.

— ROMANS 8:38-39

~

APRIL 18

"And nothing past"

There is one time a new creation should give up hope, one thing we can give up on: we can *never* change our past. For us to try and change our past is to drag around an unnecessary burden, like a man who drags around boulders. Weights tie us down and limit life. Why not cut them loose and live lightly and freely?

God has forgiven you. Believe and receive it, and move on. Forgive *yourself*, and move on! Life is too short to be lived with unnecessary burdens. Receive God's freedom today and *free yourself!*

As far as the east is from the west,
    So far has He removed our transgressions from us.

— PSALM 103:12

APRIL 19

"Nor things to come"

Why worry about what *might* happen? We cannot see what tomorrow brings. There is only One who sees and knows—and He cares about our every need. When we constantly worry about the necessities of life we play right into the hands and schemes of the enemy. God is provider, and He sees and *meets* our needs before we even know we have them. God has our back!

Let us practice trusting that truth today. Go about your work and business and do all you do as unto the Lord, and trust Him to provide for the necessities of life. Life is too precious to be burdened with unnecessary worry. Let God be God and you be His child today. His throne is not big enough for the both of you!

> For this reason I say to you, do not be worried about your life, as to what you will eat or what you will drink; nor for your body, as to what you will put on. Is not life more than food, and the body more than clothing? Look at the birds of the air, that they do not sow, nor reap nor gather into barns, and yet your heavenly Father feeds them. Are you not worth much more than they? And who of you by being worried can add a single hour to his life?
>
> — MATTHEW 6:25-27

APRIL 20

"These things won't last"

The enemy always wants the things that worry us to be constantly before us. He wants to do nothing but stir up a constant storm in our minds that keep us from focusing on the things of God. He desires nothing less than getting us to take matters into our own hands. I have good news for you. We can speak "Peace, be still" to those storms by walking in simple faith and by seeing even the little worries from the King's perspective. Reality is this: God is constant, regardless of the storms of our lives.

Trust Him in even the small matters today and effectively speak peace to the storms.

> Leaving the crowd, they took Him along with them in the boat, just as He was; and other boats were with Him. And there arose a fierce gale of wind, and the waves were breaking over the boat so much that the boat was already filling up. Jesus Himself was in the stern, asleep on the cushion; and they woke Him and said to Him, "Teacher, do You not care that we are perishing?" And He got up and rebuked the wind and said to the sea, "Hush, be still." And the wind died down and it became perfectly calm.
>
> — MARK 4:36-39

APRIL 21

"Not even death…Not even life can separate Your love from my life"

Today, let's think about the things we worry about in light of eternity. What will matter once we step across death's door and into the glorious revelation of eternity with God? None of those worries will matter! Friends, we live in eternity *now*. At least, that should be our attitude. When we recognize that this earth is simply a place we are passing through to get to glory, the things that cause us so much grief and concern will lose their power to control our lives. Do we need food, clothing, and shelter? You bet. Have you truly ever seen the righteous forsaken? I have not. God is faithful and will meet all our needs as we walk and work in relationship with Him. Even death loses its dark power over us when we *live* our lives in intimacy with God through Christ.

Really live today. Trust God.

And my God will supply all your needs according to His riches in glory in Christ Jesus.

— PHILIPPIANS 4:19

APRIL 22

"All the clouds and darkest nights seem to vanish from my sight"

This morning, my son and I drove through the thick fog of a California morning. We could see very little of the beautiful scenery, only the things that were within 150 feet of the vehicle. By faith, we knew there were majestic mountains nearby. By faith, we knew we could get to our destination, albeit a more slowly than we had hoped. After our event, we walked outside into a bright, sunny sky! What had happened? The winds had begun to blow and the sun had begun to pound the fog, and it was soon driven away revealing all we had missed before!

Our walk with God can be like that at times, but he is always about our best—even when we cannot see. He is always there, blowing in like the wind and permeating the darkness of our lives with the glorious light of His Son.

Walk in that light today!

If we say that we have fellowship with Him and yet walk in the darkness, we lie and do not practice the truth; but if we walk in the Light as He Himself is in the Light, we have fellowship with one another, and the blood of Jesus His Son cleanses us from all sin.

— 1 JOHN 1:6-7

APRIL 23

"Every ripple seems to calm as You draw near"

Have you ever been around someone so confident in their abilities—so proven as a problem solver—that the minute they walk into a chaotic situation, everyone immediately calms down? As children, we can experience that kind of assurance when we face a new trial. As our dad or mom walked into the conflict, the conflict immediately subsided. Good news, our God is always ready, willing, and able to walk into the conflicts and chaos of our lives—and bring His peace to the situation.

When conflict arises today—and it will—choose to cry out to your Father and allow Him access to your heart and mind, and watch the peace flood in!

> But as for me, the nearness of God is my good;
> I have made the Lord God my refuge,
> That I may tell of all Your works.

> — PSALM 73:28

APRIL 24

"As temptations come my way I will be Your willing clay"

Temptation was never meant to define us. None of us get to choose what we are tempted by, but *in Christ* we have been given the ability to choose to not walk into that temptation. Temptation is simply an opportunity to walk in even deeper intimacy with Christ. The enemy fights hard for your mind. Why else would he be tempting you unless He *knows* the Lord has something amazing waiting for you?

Today, walk into the amazing potential of your relationship with God each and every time temptation comes your way. Temptation will lose its power to deceive you and will actually become a joy as it becomes a reminder to seek hard after your God! Rather than say to the temptation, "What is it?" Allow the temptation to direct you to Father and ask Him, "What is it, Lord?"

And without faith it is impossible to please Him, for he who comes to God must believe that He is and that He is a rewarder of those who seek Him.

— HEBREWS 11:6

APRIL 25

"Take this vessel, Lord, and make me crystal clear"

Life is like a river. Water flows *through* the river. That river receives life from its tributaries and it, in turn, gives that life away to all it flows to. If that river becomes dammed, it loses its power and the flow stops. The water stagnates and the life ebbs quickly from it. We need to be cleansed daily in order to keep the river of our hearts and minds open to the ways of the Lord and to the needs of those around us. If we are to be vessels the Lord—and His love and power—can flow right through, we need to clear our consciences of sin and wrong attitudes.

Spend time each day pouring out your failings and weaknesses and bad attitudes to the Lord. It doesn't take long, He instantly forgives, and we walk away as vessels of power and love!

Create in me a clean heart, O God,
   And renew a steadfast spirit within me.

— PSALM 51:10

"But as for me I shall sing of Thy strength and lovingkindness"

Listen to the song "But As For Me" from the album *We Are The Army*.

But as for me I shall sing of Thy strength and loving kindness!
But as for me I shall sing of thy strength and love for me!

You're a Great God Lord Jesus!
You're my Stronghold,
You're my Strength!

You're a Great God Lord Jesus!
You're my Fortress!
You're my Shepherd!

Regardless of what my circumstances are, I *will* praise God. And when I feel too weak or overwhelmed to do even that, I will call upon my friends who walk toward God with me to help me keep praising God no matter what! There is such power in praise because God inhabits—dwells in and upon—the praise of His people! Worshiping our God puts our circumstances in proper perspective. When we worship and praise God, we are telling our own souls to be still and know God is in control, we are telling the enemy we are onto his schemes and we walk in victory—we are exalting our Creator and walking in healing intimacy with Him.

But as for me, I *shall* sing of His strength and lovingkindness. Do the same all day long today as you have need.

But as for me, by Your abundant lovingkindness I will enter Your house,

At Your holy temple I will bow in reverence for You.

— PSALM 5:7

Because Your lovingkindness is better than life,

My lips will praise You.

— PSALM 63:3

∽

APRIL 27

"But as for me I shall sing of Thy strength and love for me"

When we walk with the Lord, we do not compare ourselves to others. If someone else chooses to stay where they are spiritually, I cannot allow their lack of self-determination to keep me from going further in and higher up in my relationship with Christ. Even if no one else goes with me on my journey I will still declare His strength and love in my life, and live like I believe it to be reality, even if no one else chooses to live in my reality. We do not stop relating to people who are not where we are. We continue to love others while we keep our eyes and hearts focused on Jesus, without condemnation but with humility. Regardless of whether anyone goes with me, I walk with Christ.

Walk as one determined to know Him today.

You are the God who works wonders;

You have made known Your strength among the peoples.

APRIL 28

"You're a great God, Lord Jesus!"

God the Father, God the Spirit, and God the Son—Jesus—are one! How this could be is beyond my wildest imagination. God is a mystery to me in so many ways, but it is that very desire to unravel—to know—the mystery He is that keeps me pursuing Him! With each discovery of some new facet of His nature and character I am renewed and strengthened in my life. His mercy is unthinkable. His grace is unfathomable. His wisdom is too grand to take it all in. His love is beyond human capacity to measure.

Spend time seeking to unravel the mystery of God as you walk relationally with Him today. Be ready to be overwhelmed!

I am no longer in the world; and yet they themselves are in the world, and I come to You. Holy Father, keep them in Your name, the name which You have given Me, that they may be one even as We are.

— JOHN 17:11

APRIL 29

"You're my stronghold!"

A stronghold is a place where the enemy has dug into our lives and taken up residence, filling our minds with lies that we cannot seem to shake. When we recognize the lies, it is important that we completely eradicate those strongholds of the lies and replace those lies with the truth. In reality, we must make the Lord our stronghold in place of the enemy! In Christ—as a new creation—I am who Father says I am. He is like a mighty fortress where I can run and be safe, no matter *what* I am going through.

Meditate today on the reality that God is your stronghold—a mighty fortress where you can be safe. *Live* there!

> The Lord is my rock and my fortress and my deliverer,
>> My God, my rock, in whom I take refuge;
>> My shield and the horn of my salvation, my stronghold.

> — PSALM 18:2

APRIL 30

"You're my strength!"

God has imbued each and every person with an innate strength: the strength to desire life, to live! Every person is born a fighter to some extent. The enemy has a way of knocking us to our knees and believing we cannot be strong.

Life itself has a way of humbling the heart of prideful man to a certain degree. Yet even man's greatest strength is not enough to save and satisfy the soul. Our strength was given to be poured out in pursuit of God—and every man pursues God, even if they do not know it! We all want to know who we are and why we are here. Who put that in us? God Himself.

Let us find our greatest strength today by seeking Him, and once there, find supernatural strength by confessing our ultimate weakness without and apart from Him. As a result, we. Can find power to overcome any and all circumstances in this life as we live in *His* strength!

My flesh and my heart may fail,
    But God is the strength of my heart and my portion forever.

— PSALM 73:26

MAY

MAY 1

"You're a great God, Lord Jesus!"

There are many gods of this world that vie for our attention and allegiance. Money can be a god. Things can be our god. Fame and popularity can be gods. Anything that has our heart —anything we live for—is our god to a certain degree. The reality is that there is only one God and His name is Jehovah, Jesus, Holy Spirit! When we place our focus on *Him* all earthly things fall into their proper places in our lives. Money becomes a resource for the Kingdom. Possessions become resources for the Kingdom. Even a man's fame or popularity can be a resource for the Kingdom of God.

Choose you this day who you will serve, and then *live* your life accordingly, with great joy and purpose.

For the grace of God has appeared, bringing salvation to all men, instructing us to deny ungodliness and worldly desires and to live sensibly, righteously and godly in the present age, looking for the blessed hope and the appearing of the glory of our great God and Savior, Christ Jesus.

— TITUS 2:11-13

MAY 2

"You're my fortress!"

A fortress is a place of safety. A fortress is a place of strength. A fortress is a place where life can go on even when the inhabitants of that fortress are under constant siege from the enemy. When life leaves us feeling vulnerable, we have a place—a fortress like no other—where we can run and be safe. It is up to us to step, by faith, into the safety of The Fortress. When we feel too weak to keep up the battle for our minds, the Lord is a fortress where we can find peace for our weariness. When we feel that life is being sucked right out of us due to trials and circumstances, we have a fortress where all of those circumstances and trials can be seen from the King's point of view.

Let us consciously and intentionally live from the safety of our Fortress today.

The name of the Lord is a strong tower;
  The righteous runs into it and is safe.

— PROVERBS 18:10

MAY 3

"You're my strength!"

Because of sin, we go through periods where we think we are the reason for our own success. Reality is this: it is God and others that help us get to where we are. Plain and simple. It is futile to think that we alone are the sole strength of our own life. When we boil life down to its lowest common denominators we find that *He* is God, and we are not. When we understand that, we have a solid foundation from which to live our lives.

Live today with that simple reality and let the power of that truth permeate all you think, say, and do. Allow God to truly be the strength of your life.

> The Lord is my light and my salvation;
> Whom shall I fear?
> The Lord is the defense of my life;
> Whom shall I dread?

— PSALM 27:1

MAY 4

"I will glory in my weakness"

In God's economy, nothing is wasted if we bring it to Him in honest confession. He has the ability, power, and creativity to take even our failures and make something good out of

115

them. He can take the ashes of our lives and make something beautiful from them. But as long as we keep those things—whatever they may be—bottled up inside, we effectively hinder the power, work, and creativity of God. We resist His grace! When we realize the power of honest confession and open our souls completely to Him, we witness His glory as He takes what we see as wasted and makes something valuable of it.

Let us ponder these thoughts today and truly glory in our weakness, that He may be strong in us!

> And He has said to me, "My grace is sufficient for you, for power is perfected in weakness." Most gladly, therefore, I will rather boast about my weaknesses, so that the power of Christ may dwell in me.

> — 2 CORINTHIANS 12:9

MAY 5

"I will boast in Your might"

When we recognize that it is the power of God which gives us our every breath (He is the reason we even exist), then we have a proper focus for how to live our lives. The enemy wants us to walk around in shame—debilitated and in defeat due to our sin. God sent a Redeemer to rescue and deliver us from sin, and to restore us to right standing with our Maker. This is the basis of our victory. Sin is dealt with and forgiven. We are cleansed, born again, and raised to walk in the power of our true identity as new creations!

Boast in the power and might of our God who has such

love for us! He is mighty in forgiveness, mighty in redemption, mighty in love! Let us boast in our God today!

> Therefore I am well content with weaknesses, with insults, with distresses, with persecutions, with difficulties, for Christ's sake; for when I am weak, then I am strong.

> — 2 CORINTHIANS 12:10

MAY 6

> *"For I have found in my weakness that You will be the strength of my life"*

When I am weak, then He is strong. In simple truth, it is when we step off of the throne of our own hearts and allow the Lord to sit there—rightfully so—that we find the power of God to live an abundant life, regardless of the circumstances that come our way. Let us take time today to allow the King to have His rightful place in our hearts that we might be conduits of all He is to those around us. In doing so, we are being who He re-created us to be: new creations and vessels of honor that exude His glory and power *just by recognizing our identity and living it out!*

Recognize your need today and watch the power of God invade all you face.

> The Lord is my rock and my fortress and my deliverer,
> My God, my rock, in whom I take refuge;
> My shield and the horn of my salvation, my stronghold.

> — PSALM 18:2

MAY 7

"You are the strength of my life"

The place where our weakness meets the realization that we cannot save ourselves is the place where we find deep intimacy with God. Like a child that cannot cleanse his own wounds, console his own soul, or comfort his own sorrow, we must approach the Father in the reality of our need. It is in that place of honesty where we find His grace—the power to live life joyfully and abundantly in spite of the circumstances.

Go to that place often today, receive all the grace you need, and enjoy your life abundantly!

> The thief comes only to steal and kill and destroy; I came that they may have life, and have *it* abundantly.
>
> — JOHN 10:10

MAY 8

"You are my song"

A song is a series of notes that form a melody, usually having words and a definite form. Songs have the power to evoke certain emotions—to bring solace to a weary soul. Our God is like the greatest song ever written. We can hear Him singing His presence wherever we find ourselves, regardless of the severity of the things we face. Songs are great conduits of relationship and conveyors of joy. Our God is like that. He sings His desire to know us in a constantly resounding melody. Knowing He is singing His presence to us is the basis of our joy! We are never alone!

Be listening for His song today whether you "hear" it melodically or in the simple grace of His presence. Receive the peace and joy He offers and be blessed.

> Behold, God is my salvation,
>> I will trust and not be afraid;
>> For the Lord God is my strength and song,
>> And He has become my salvation.

— ISAIAH 12:2

MAY 9

"You are the strength of my life"

Take time to look back on the last few days of your life. Allow the Holy Spirit to prompt you to see evidence of God's strength in your life that you may not have noticed. Each time something comes to your remembrance, give God thanks. In doing so, you are accomplishing relationship in a very foundational way. You are saying to God, "I am weak but You are strong," and He is saying, "Child, I am with you constantly because I love you so much." Remember to allow Him to show you *His* perspective on even the hard and hurtful things you may have had to endure. Not only is our God mighty to save, but He is *always* good and desires only our best.

And we know that God causes all things to work together for

good to those who love God, to those who are called according to His purpose.

— ROMANS 8:28

MAY 10

"When I am weak, You are strong"

One way to look at the statement, "When I am weak, He is strong," is to simply recognize the most basic of truths: He is God and we are not! It does not matter how gifted or talented we are, He is the one who gave us our gifts and talents. It does not matter how intellectual we are, He is the one who gave us our intellect. It doesn't even matter how mature we become in this life, He is the one who has woven the very fabric of our identity and brought us to where we are—whether we realize it or not!

Spend time today simply pondering the extent of who He is and the wonder of what that means for you. In your frailty discover His strength.

The Lord is my light and my salvation;
Whom shall I fear?
The Lord is the defense of my life;
Whom shall I dread?

— PSALM 27:1

MAY 11

"You are the strength of my life"

Are there any areas of your life where you feel weak today? Wisdom is learning to see life and its circumstances from God's point of view. Are you having trouble with finances? Have you asked the Lord to show you what He sees? Perhaps there is an area of financial creativity you haven't seen or a new way to bring revenue into your life from a resource you never thought of before. Perhaps you feel weak in the area of relating to a family member. What does that relationship look like from God's point of view? Perhaps, you have not seen an insight that may resolve the conflict or may bring about deeper intimacy.

Seek God in your weakness, see what He sees, and find His strength in the process.

> Behold, I will do something new,
>> Now it will spring forth;
>> Will you not be aware of it?
>> I will even make a roadway in the wilderness,
>> Rivers in the desert.

— ISAIAH 43:19

MAY 12

"You are my song"

God's Word is full of admonitions to sing to and make

melody in our hearts to the Lord. Have you ever wondered why that is? My personal belief is that singing requires our entire being to be focused toward God. And when our focus is toward God the enemy has no ground on which to plant the seeds of his subtle lies! Singing to God requires our thoughts to be taken captive. Singing requires an emotional response. Singing requires our physical participation. To sing to God is to practice devotion and intimacy and relationship to and with the God who sings over us! Notice that we are never required to have a "good" voice, just to make a joyful noise to Him!

Do you want victory over the lies of the enemy? Sing to God! Do you want greater intimacy with your Maker? Sing to Him!

> O come, let us sing for joy to the Lord,
>> Let us shout joyfully to the rock of our salvation.

> — PSALM 95:1

MAY 13

"When I am weak I will praise and be strong"

Often, the very best time for us to sing our praise to God is the time when we feel the most weak and frail! The wonderful paradox of that reality is that by simply focusing our entire being on God with a song, we effectively shut down the lies of the enemy that weigh us down with doubt, fear, and worry. It is when we are consumed in praise for God that we see those fears and doubts and worries for what they truly are: opportunities to cry out for and receive the grace of God.

Do not be fooled by the subtle schemes of the enemy today. See past his smokescreen to the wonderful reality of God's point of view on your life. Live in that place of victory today.

Wait for the Lord;
>   Be strong and let your heart take courage;
>   Yes, wait for the Lord.

— PSALM 27:14

MAY 14

"When I'm weak You're my strength and my song"

The quickest way to the realization of God's presence is to acknowledge our need of Him. No matter how mature we become in the Lord, we still have need of His power. Regardless of how adept we become at seeing life from His perspective, we still need His strength. Remember, He is God and we are not! It is in this most basic realization—that apart from His love, grace, and mercy we would be hopeless—that we find our greatest strength. To the world, it may seem weakness to simply know He is with us through thick and thin, that He has our back no matter what, that He desires rich and life-sustaining relationship with us. But we know better. We know that our truest and greatest strength lies in that reality.

Live that reality today and allow the Lord to be your strength and song!

The Lord is my strength and song,
>   And He has become my salvation;

This is my God, and I will praise Him;
My father's God, and I will extol Him.

— EXODUS 15:2

MAY 15

"Lord, please keep me in weakness"

I often pray, "Lord, please keep me in weakness." What do I mean by that? Such a prayer is simply my way of submitting my soul and will to *His* will by acknowledging my great and desperate need for Him in my life. Even though I know He will never leave me or forsake me, I desire a living and breathing relationship with Him—a relationship built on two-way communication and communion. As I bare my soul to Him, He pours His life into me. As I confess my weakness to Him, He pours His love and strength into me. What the world calls weak, He calls strong. I need my God—at all times. I need my God.

Practice this simple reality today. Be weak and find your true strength.

Because the foolishness of God is wiser than men, and the weakness of God is stronger than men.

— 1 CORINTHIANS 1:25

MAY 16

"Melt my heart in Your light"

Life has a way of hardening our hearts. Sometimes it is easier to grow numb and feel nothing than to deal with the pain life can bring. When our hearts grow hard, we tend to hide things that are best dealt with in the light of truth. Far too often I allow the cares of this world to burden my soul rather than simply dealing with them as they arise. Before long I find myself weighed down, growing numb, and hiding from God and others. The remedy? Open, honest confession, and inner cleansing of my heart and mind!

Today, practice the presence of God by simply confessing your needs—whatever they might be. A soft heart is much more pliable and useful to the kingdom than one that is hard and unfeeling. Have your cares melted away by the love of God today!

> Light is sown like seed for the righteous
>> And gladness for the upright in heart.
>> Be glad in the Lord, you righteous ones,
>> And give thanks to His holy name.

— PSALM 97:11-12

MAY 17

"Fill me Lord, with Your brokenness"

To know Christ is to also identify with His suffering. He came to meet the needs of people, to bear the burden of their sin and sorrow, and to ultimately make a way for redemption. He bore our grief and suffered our shame. He made a way to bridge the gap between us and our God. When we become new creations in Christ, we are transformed in our very nature from sinner to saint! As one of God's new creations, we are empowered to do the work of ministry—just like Christ came to do. As ministers of the love of God, we are capable of helping bear the burdens of those around us and becoming agents of God's redeeming love.

Be sensitive to the brokenness of those around you today, and be prepared to minister the healing power of His love.

> The sacrifices of God are a broken spirit;
>   A broken and a contrite heart, O God,
>   You will not despise.

— PSALM 51:17

MAY 18

"Pour through me with the strength of Your Life"

Life flows freely in our relationship with God when we open our hearts to Him and He opens His heart to us. It is when we allow sin to cloud our vision, or when we allow the deception of the enemy to be our focus, that the flow of that relationship is blocked. It is of vital importance to our lives — our abundant lives—that we keep the flow open. That flow is our strength!

Spend time today allowing the Lord to reveal any sin or deception you are walking in. If any is revealed, repent, put on the truth, and go on!

Then the lame will leap like a deer,
And the tongue of the mute will shout for joy.
For waters will break forth in the wilderness
And streams in the Arabah [desert].

— ISAIAH 35:6

MAY 19

"I will worship You, Jesus"

Worship is a mighty tool in the hands and heart of the believer. Worship focuses our attention on our Maker. Worship quiets the soul and causes the enemy to flee. Worship brings an awareness of the deepest reality of all—a living, vital relationship with our God.

Worship Him today in thought. Worship Him today in attitude. Worship Him today in spirit. Worship Him today in song. Worship Him today in action. Worship Him with emotion. Worship Him in quiet stillness. Worship Him and be consumed with His presence and love—regardless of the busyness of your day. He will meet you where your heart worships.

For though the Lord is exalted,
> Yet He regards the lowly,
> But the haughty He knows from afar.

— PSALM 138:6

MAY 20

"I will bow in Your sight"

To bow down to someone is to show respect and honor. To bow down to someone is to humble oneself. When we bow down to our God, we are submitting our life to Him in humility, realizing that apart from Him we would be lost, apart from Him we would be dead, apart from Him we would be without hope. Life without Him is futile and joyless. Spend time today bowing in heart, mind, attitude, and spirit. Allow Him to reveal Himself to you in unexpected ways. In other words, be expecting to see His handiwork when you humble yourself before Him.

> Come, let us worship and bow down,
> Let us kneel before the Lord our Maker.

— PSALM 95:6

MAY 21

"For power is perfected in weakness!"

How is it possible that power could be perfected in weakness? In today's culture, power is what everyone seems to be after. People seek power at any cost and wind up losing everything in the process. Could it be that true power lies in the humble heart of a servant? When we realize that all power and authority comes from our Maker, we begin to understand, utilize, and operate in the power of that reality. It is God, and His use of other people in our lives, that has given us any success or power whatsoever. The humble heart who realizes its need for God — no matter how mature and healthy it becomes — stays strong.

Be strong today by admitting your need for the Living God.

And He has said to me, "My grace is sufficient for you, for power is perfected in weakness." Most gladly, therefore, I will rather boast about my weaknesses, so that the power of Christ may dwell in me.

— 2 CORINTHIANS 12:9

MAY 22

"I know that power is perfected in weakness!"

Begin today by practicing the strength of weakness — humbling yourself before God. Thank Him for saving you from your depraved life of sin. Bow before Him as you confess your need for Him today. Submit your entire being to the power of His love and be embraced by that powerful force throughout the day. Simply practice His presence by believing He is there even when you feel or sense nothing. Practice His power by recognizing your need for Him regardless of how mature you think you are. Revel in His goodness and love for you, and watch the power of His love energize your entire being. Enjoy your "weakness" today!

> Therefore I am well content with weaknesses, with insults, with distresses, with persecutions, with difficulties, for Christ's sake; for when I am weak, then I am strong.
>
> — 2 CORINTHIANS 12:10

MAY 23

"Oh, Lord, power is perfected in weakness!"

If power is truly perfected in weakness it stands to reason that the most powerful are those who realize their state and walk in humility with the Lord. It was, after all, the Servant of All who set the world on its head with His resurrection! Jesus came to serve, humbling Himself by becoming one of us! Jesus even washed the feet of those who served *Him!* This was the King of Kings doing the work of a humble servant! How could that be? This was the God of the Universe, Redeemer of Mankind, who suffered a criminal's death to save us from our sin! Yet, this was the One who rose in power, conquering death and defeating sin!

Let us be like Him today. Let us walk in humility, serving God and serving those around us, laying down our lives just as He laid down His.

Greater love has no one than this, that one lay down his life for his friends.

— JOHN 15:13

MAY 24

"By Your blood You're the strength of my life!"

Without the life-giving blood that flows through our physical bodies, we would not live. It is the same in our spiritual lives. Without the life-giving blood of Jesus Christ, we would not be able to survive! I was once physically wounded and, during the early phases of my recovery, told to make the wound bleed as much as possible to help it close properly. Why? Because the blood would bring nutrients necessary for healing, and the wound would heal faster by doing so! By the blood of Jesus our sins are cleansed. By the blood of Jesus we are redeemed. By the blood of Jesus we overcome the enemy. By the blood of Jesus we are restored to right relationship with God. By the blood of Jesus our spiritual wounds are healed.

Find strength in the blood of Jesus today!

But now in Christ Jesus you who formerly were far off have been brought near by the blood of Christ.

— EPHESIANS 2:13

MAY 25

"The world's mistaken but we must stand"

Listen to "The World's Mistaken" from the album *We Are The Army*.

The world's mistaken — but we must stand!
By the Spirit, drive the enemy from the land!
For Satan's seeking the Kingdom land!
But he is defeated by the Lord's own mighty hand!

The world's mistaken — but we must stand!
By the Spirit, drive the enemy from the land!
For Satan's seeking the Kingdom land!
But he is defeated by the Lord's own mighty hand!

The Lord's own mighty hand!

There is so much pressure from the world to conform to its ways. Real wisdom is seeing life from God's perspective rather than from the world's. The world tends to view things from the vantage point of man being the highest form of intelligence. It does not take long to look at history and see how far short mankind's wisdom falls: failed economic systems, failed social policies, wars, genocide, torture, slavery, sex trafficking. Fame and beauty fade. Fortunes are lost over night. Man knows best? I don't think so. Even though the wisdom of God may seem foolish to the world, it is the way to life.

Today, do not be conformed to the lies of the world. God

has grace to help you swim against the flow! Stand firm, see life from the King's point of view, and live!

> And do not be conformed to this world, but be transformed by the renewing of your mind, so that you may prove what the will of God is, that which is good and acceptable and perfect.
>
> — ROMANS 12:2

MAY 26

"By the Spirit drive the enemy from the land"

There are practical things we can do to drive the enemy from our thoughts. We can commit God's Word to memory and use it to put down the enemy's lies. We can worship God, fill our minds with holy thoughts, and create an atmosphere where the enemy cannot stand. We can put on the full armor of God and guard our spirits with spiritual fortitude. We can avail ourselves of the blood of Jesus and remind the enemy that we belong to God. We can, and must, walk in a state of spiritual warfare and take back the ground the enemy has stolen from us and those we love.

Today, purpose to drive the enemy and his lying ways from our own hearts and minds, and intercede for others along the way.

> For though we walk in the flesh, we do not war according to the flesh, for the weapons of our warfare are not of the flesh, but divinely powerful for the destruction of fortresses. We

are destroying speculations and every lofty thing raised up against the knowledge of God, and we are taking every thought captive to the obedience of Christ.

— 2 CORINTHIANS 10:3-5

MAY 27

"For Satan's seeking the Kingdom land"

Satan's goal is to keep as many as possible out of the Kingdom of God and to make those in the Kingdom as weak and ineffectual as possible. What we, as children of the King, must realize is that we cannot be defeated! We have been given Kingdom authority and power by virtue of the blood of Jesus and by our position as joint-heirs with Christ! Whether we live or die, we win!

Today, put on the attitude of one who knows their destiny! Walk as one who knows the end of the story, regardless of the journey required to get there! Put the enemy where he belongs —under your feet!

Be of sober spirit, be on the alert. Your adversary, the devil, prowls around like a roaring lion, seeking someone to devour. But resist him, firm in your faith, knowing that the same experiences of suffering are being accomplished by your brethren who are in the world.

— 1 PETER 5:8-9

MAY 28

"But he is defeated by the Lord's own mighty hand"

Just as we know that Jesus overcame sin, death, and the enemy, we must realize that we have the same victory! Satan and his minions have been utterly defeated by the blood of Christ and the power of the resurrection. We, being *in* Christ, have been afforded that same victory over the enemy! It is when we believe that truth that we begin to walk in the power of that truth. We *are* overcomers! We are victors rather than victims! We are destined to win!

Walk as one who knows their identity and destiny today. Do not be fooled by the lies of the Deceiver. Put off the lies, put on the truth, and watch victory unfold before you today!

And they overcame him because of the blood of the Lamb and because of the word of their testimony, and they did not love their life even when faced with death.

— REVELATION 12:11

MAY 29

"We are the army shielded in the blood"

Listen to the song "We Are The Army" from the album *We Are The Army.*

We are the army shielded in the blood!

135

And we are crushing the enemy like a mighty flood!
Oh, Lord of Hosts, strong in victory!
Oh, Lord of Hosts rise up O God, in me!
For it is by the blood of the Lamb that we will stand!
By the blood of the Lamb we will stand!
By the blood of the Lamb we will stand!
By the blood of the Lamb we will stand!

When the blood of Jesus is put to use by the believer, the enemy is vanquished from our minds. Our minds are the battlefield of our lives. This is why we must learn to recognize the lies and replace them with the truth. How do we recognize the lies? By learning the truth of God's Word. By learning to know who God says he is. By learning to walk in the identities He has called us to! The blood of Jesus seals our destiny and our identity! We belong to Him and are citizens of the eternal realm of His Kingdom!

Walk as one who knows who and whose they are today!

Therefore, brethren, since we have confidence to enter the holy place by the blood of Jesus, by a new and living way which He inaugurated for us through the veil, that is, His flesh, and since we have a great priest over the house of God, let us draw near with a sincere heart in full assurance of faith, having our hearts sprinkled clean from an evil conscience and our bodies washed with pure water.

— HEBREWS 10:19-22

"And we are crushing the enemy like a mighty flood"

The enemy is defeated. His only power is that of deception. Do not allow him to deceive you today. When confronted by one of his lies, be quick to put it under your feet and declare the truth. You, as a new creation, have been granted authority over him and his lies. By appropriating the truth and by applying the power of the blood of Jesus, you are assured the victory. We do not have to settle for anything less than God's best in this life—even if the world falls apart around us. We always have a choice in any matter as to how we will respond. Even when we suffer or sorrow, we know who holds us and gives us a Solid Foundation on which to stand. By walking in the authority given us—by virtue of our citizenship in God's Kingdom—we effectively crush the enemy in our lives.

Walk as a Lie Crusher today!

We know that we are of God, and that the whole world lies in the power of the evil one. And we know that the Son of God has come, and has given us understanding so that we may know Him who is true; and we are in Him who is true, in His Son Jesus Christ. This is the true God and eternal life.

— 1 JOHN 5:19-20

"Oh, Lord of Hosts, strong in victory"

Our God is Mighty to save. Our God is mighty to deliver. Our God is mighty in victory. And because we belong to Him, we are saved, delivered, and victorious! How simple is that? Yet we often allow the lies of the enemy to divert our attention from the truth of our position in Christ. Regardless of how we feel, we win. Regardless of what others choose to do or believe, we win. Regardless of what worldly wisdom says about us, we win. Regardless of our circumstances, we win. Why do we win? Because our God has already won—and we are *His!*

Walk as one who knows they are victorious today!

Cease striving and know that I am God;
    I will be exalted among the nations,
    I will be exalted in the earth.
    The Lord of hosts is with us;
    The God of Jacob is our stronghold.

— PSALM 46:10-11

JUNE

JUNE 1

"Oh, Lord of Hosts, rise up, Oh God, in me"

God calls himself the Lord of Hosts. Those hosts include the legions of angels who serve as His messengers, and it includes the legion of saints who have died and gone to be with Him since the beginning of mankind's existence on earth. That means that we are certainly not alone. So often, the scheme of the enemy is to get us to feeling as if no one else can understand what we are going through, or to get us to feeling as if we are utterly alone. The reality is that we have a great cloud of witnesses who have paved the way for us and have gone on before us, showing us the way.

Let us put the enemy in his place today by remembering that truth. Let our faith be encouraged as we think on its grand heritage. You are just like Moses and Noah and Abraham and Peter and Paul. Be the overcomer you are born to be.

> Therefore, since we have so great a cloud of witnesses surrounding us, let us also lay aside every encumbrance and the sin which so easily entangles us, and let us run with endurance the race that is set before us, fixing our eyes on Jesus, the author and perfecter of faith, who for the joy set before Him endured the cross, despising the shame, and has sat down at the right hand of the throne of God.
>
> — HEBREWS 12:1-2

~

JUNE 2

"For it is by the blood of the Lamb that we will stand"

We are guaranteed the victory over sin, death, and the lies of the enemy by virtue of the blood of Jesus Christ. His blood cleanses us from all sin. His blood paid our sin-debt. His blood endows us with resurrection power and a brand new identity. When the lies of the enemy come, let us plead the blood of Jesus over our minds and walk in the victory that truth brings. We overcome the enemy by the fact that we have been purchased by Jesus Christ's blood and we belong to *the* Victor.

Be who you were signed sealed, and delivered to be! Be a new creation today!

And they overcame him because of the blood of the Lamb

and because of the word of their testimony, and they did not love their life even when faced with death.

— REVELATION 12:11

JUNE 3

"By the blood of the Lamb we will stand"

Let us meditate today on the reality of all that the blood of Christ means to us as believers. If His blood cleanses us, are we acting as ones who believe they have been cleansed? If His blood has purchased us, do our attitudes reflect the reality of who we belong to? If His blood secures our victory over the lies of the enemy, are we walking in the power of that truth today?

Today, allow the Holy Spirit to reveal greater depths of the power of the blood of Christ. And then put the things revealed into your personal arsenal of truth to wage war against the lies of the enemy. You *are* a victor today!

But now in Christ Jesus the blood of Christ has brought you who formerly were far off near.

— EPHESIANS 2:13

JUNE 4

"Let the church now rise and storm the gates of Hell"

Why do we fear the mention of sin or Hell or the existence of Satan? Far too often, we allow culture to affect us rather than the other way around. It is far easier to be politically correct than to make waves. We, as the church—the body of Christ—must stand, assume, and walk in our true identity, and embrace our destiny. We are called to do the work of ministry. We are called to make disciples. We are called to be salt and light. As long as we fear what others may think or say or do should we assume our destiny, as long as we are cowed by the lies of the enemy, then we will be watered down and of little effect.

We have been given the keys to defeating the enemy and his scheming lies. Let us storm the gates of Hell today in thought, attitude, and action.

> I also say to you that you are Peter, and upon this rock I will build My church; and the gates of Hades will not overpower it. I will give you the keys of the kingdom of heaven; and whatever you bind on earth shall have been bound in heaven, and whatever you loose on earth shall have been loosed in heaven.
>
> — MATTHEW 16:18-19

JUNE 5

"Let the people rejoice! Their mighty praises swell!"

As believers, one of the greatest weapons we have been given for storming the gates of Hell is the simple act of praise! When we lift up, exalt, extol, and declare our gratitude for God in thought, attitude, and action, we literally put the enemy to flight while simultaneously taking our own thoughts captive to the obedience of Christ! Why would we resist praising our God? In my relationship with my wife, I did not limit my love and praise to our courting days or wedding day. I continue that love and praise because it is a source of life to our relationship! If I did not continue to nurture that relationship it would wither and die. Just as in my marriage relationship, I desire life with my Savior and Lord!

Let us praise God today and rejoice in all He has done. Then, sit back and watch abundant life be the result.

Let the high praises of God be in their mouth,
And a two-edged sword in their hand,
To execute vengeance on the nations
And punishment on the peoples,
To bind their kings with chains
And their nobles with fetters of iron,
To execute on them the judgment written;
This is an honor for all His godly ones.
Praise the Lord!

— PSALM 149:6-9

JUNE 6

"Let the army arise and let your praise go forth"

There were times, in the days of Moses and Joshua, when the Lord sent out his armies with worshipers leading the way! I think we should take a clue from that in our own battles. We often allow the circumstances of life to determine our thoughts, our attitudes, and subsequently, our actions. Is that God's best? No! Our attitudes affect everything about us. Why would we ever allow the enemy to determine our attitude? But that is effectively what we do when we allow our attitudes to be determined by our circumstances—we play right into the trap of the Liar. We can counter that scheme by determining ahead of time, by having a plan of attack, how we will respond when circumstances are less than stellar. Let us worship and praise our God in spite of the storms, in spite of our feelings, in spite of the lies of the enemy. This will affect our attitudes and help usher in peace in the storm, comfort for our broken hearts, and truth the defeat the Liar.

Rise up and lead God's army with praise today!

So the people shouted, and priests blew the trumpets; and when the people heard the sound of the trumpet, the people shouted with a great shout and the wall fell down flat, so that the people went up into the city, every man straight ahead, and they took the city.

— JOSHUA 6:20

JUNE 7

"For Jesus is the mighty Lord"

We are assured our victory over the enemy simply because of the blood and resurrection of Jesus Christ! Since we are assured of this triumph, we should think accordingly, we should have victory as an attitude, and we should act as those who know they are victorious!

Focus today on simply being a joint-heir with the Victor. Think thoughts that lead to victory. Have the attitude of one who knows, when all is said and done, who wins. Today, walk, talk, and minister to those around you as one who knows the power of their victory and choose to be victorious, regardless of your circumstances.

> The wicked are overthrown and are no more,
> But the house of the righteous will stand.

— PROVERBS 12:7

JUNE 8

"Storm the gates of Hell"

Sometimes it feels like people are our enemy, especially when they hurt us. But rest assured, the enemy and his lies are always behind discord. We must be quick to see such episodes of hurt from the King's perspective, otherwise bitterness will rule the day. Even when our feelings are legitimate, we have the ability to receive God's grace, put on forgiveness, and put the enemy in his place — under our feet.

Today, let us focus our attitudes and thoughts on the reality that the enemy is the enemy. Do not allow him to throw up smokescreens to divert our focus. Let us storm the gates of Hell with the truth of God's perspective. Worship God no matter what!

> I also say to you that you are Peter, and upon this rock I will build My church; and the gates of Hades will not overpower it. I will give you the keys of the kingdom of heaven; and whatever you bind on earth shall have been bound in heaven, and whatever you loose on earth shall have been loosed in heaven.
>
> — MATTHEW 16:18-19

JUNE 9

"Break the chains of sin"

When we constantly believe the lies of the enemy, he is able to keep us in chains — right where he wants us. We cannot afford to forget that his only power is that of deception. This means that we must be people of the truth. What is truth? Jesus is ultimate truth. He is *the* Word of God in flesh! It is by the truth of our own testimony of redemption that we overcome the Liar. It is by the truth of the redeeming blood of Jesus that we overcome the Deceiver. It is by walking intimately with Jesus that we overcome the Enemy of God.

Tired of the chains that come against your liberty in Christ?

Put on the *truth* and watch them break apart! Focus on God's Word today and be free.

> And they overcame him because of the blood of the Lamb and because of the word of their testimony, and they did not love their life even when faced with death.

— REVELATION 12:11

JUNE 10

"Storm the gates of Hell"

One of the best ways to overcome the lies of the enemy is to remind him—and yourself—who you are in Christ. You are an overcomer. You are a royal priest in the Kingdom. You are victorious. You are the righteousness of God by virtue of the blood of Jesus. You are a man or woman of peace. You are forgiven. You are chosen by God. You are a pearl of great price. You were wanted, *are* wanted. You are a joint heir with Christ. You are precious to Him. You are loved beyond measure. You have the ability to commune with God anywhere at any time under any circumstance!

Do you want to defeat the enemy? The battleground is in your mind. Use the weapons of your warfare—begin with the truth of who He is and who you are because of who He is!

> "For I know the plans that I have for you," declares the Lord, "Plans for welfare and not for calamity to give you a future and a hope."

— JEREMIAH 29:11

JUNE 11

"Shine your light within the gates of Hell"

The enemy is lord of darkness. He tries to cover our hearts and minds and very existence with darkness. His goal is to get us so consumed with darkness that we believe it is light! To live and exist in darkness is to live and exist in a constant state of death and despair and hopelessness. But there is a way out of the darkness—even for believers who fall into moments of darkness. Jesus is the Light of the world! We have instant and direct access to Him in the midst of any darkness. To live a healthy spiritual life, we must walk in the Light of Life. We must walk in intimacy—open honest communion—with our Savior.

Spend time today simply asking Him to expose any darkness in us and to bathe that area of deception with the cleansing, freeing power of His Light. Use the Word of God against the darkness.

While I am in the world, I am the Light of the world.

— JOHN 9:5

JUNE 12

"Let the Word go forth on the piercing praise of a two-edged sword"

Memorizing God's Word is an effective weapon against the

Enemy, but we do not have to have massive portions of Scripture memorized in order to come against the enemy effectively! Do not allow the Liar to incapacitate you with feelings of inadequacy in this area! When I feel bombarded by the lies of the Enemy, I do not cower in fear just because I cannot remember a passage verbatim! The concept—the meat of the truth—is mighty! I can remember that God is love! I can remember that Jesus wins over sin and death. I can remember that I am redeemed and that Jesus is my Redeemer! I can remember that I am filled with the Holy Spirit and have power over the Deceiver! I use the Word of God even when I cannot remember the exact portion I am calling into play!

Use the Word today. Even the smallest portion is enough to push back the lies and the Liar!

And the devil said to Him, "If You are the Son of God, tell this stone to become bread." And Jesus answered him, "It is written, 'Man shall not live on bread alone."

— LUKE 4:3-4

For the word of God is living and active and sharper than any two-edged sword, and piercing as far as the division of soul and spirit, of both joints and marrow, and able to judge the thoughts and intentions of the heart.

— HEBREWS 4:12

JUNE 13

"Let the army arise and let your praise go forth"

I have said this often—and you are probably getting tired of it—but worship is one of the most effective weapons against the enemy, especially in the battlefield of our mind. Worship requires my entire being. I worship with my thoughts. I express those thoughts out loud in song or word and physical expression. I use my emotions to express my heart to God on an emotional level. To worship God requires my entire being, and if I am consumed in my entire being with focus on God, I have put the Enemy under my feet where he belongs! He cannot touch my mind when it is consumed with God. He cannot sway my emotions when they are blessing God. And the greatest news is that we are not alone. God is with us constantly! But guess what. There is an army of warriors out there worshipping as well! Corporate times of worship are a blessing to us and to those we worship with!

Remember to worship regularly with like-minded believers. You'll aid in the strengthening of others and be strengthened in the process. We, the body of Christ, *are* the army of God!

Let the high praises of God be in their mouth,
    And a two-edged sword in their hand,
    To execute vengeance on the nations
    And punishment on the peoples,
    To bind their kings with chains
    And their nobles with fetters of iron,

To execute on them the judgment written;
This is an honor for all His godly ones.
Praise the Lord!

— PSALM 149:6-9

JUNE 14

"For Jesus is the mighty Lord"

What is the bottom line for any believer? To be absent from the body is to be present with Christ! Think about that. What is the worst thing that can happen to us? We can die. But even then, we are victorious! That should make us absolutely fearless! We want to be the ministers of reconciliation we have been called to be, but we often fear what others will say of us if we act like Jesus. We fear retaliation if we stand up for the sake of righteousness. We fear the repercussions should we associate with the "untouchables" of religious society—the druggies, the homosexuals, the homeless, etc. The truth is that we win no matter what!

Today, let us practice that as if we really believe it. Step out and be free. Step out and live like you really believe Jesus is mighty in you!

> If anyone hears My sayings and does not keep them, I do not judge him; for I did not come to judge the world, but to save the world.

— JOHN 12:47

JUNE 15

"You are great"

What words come to mind when you hear the word *great*? I think of something exceptional or significant in my life. I think of something good and wonderful that brings joy to my heart. Often, my thoughts go to something of immense importance or toward something that has had a huge impact on my life. When we say "God is great," we are saying all of those things and more.

Today, meditate on the greatness of God. Allow all that comes to mind to lift your heart and permeate all you think and do with a very keen awareness of the magnificent greatness of God—even in the *small* things of life!

Your way, O God, is holy;
What god is great like our God?

— PSALM 77:13

JUNE 16

"You are Lord"

We say "Jesus is Lord," but do we really allow Him that place in our lives? How often do we say one thing but think or do another? Here is the truth that always brings my heart and mind into reality concerning His Lordship—He is Lord whether I acknowledge Him or not! Just as, when receiving

His love, I must understand that He loves me whether I believe it or not, so must I do with His Lordship. What do I mean? By simply agreeing with God that He loves me, I loose chains binding my thoughts of my worthiness. By agreeing with God that Jesus is Lord, I loose chains binding my thoughts of my ability to walk away from my self-focus and self-reliance.

Spend time today thinking about the Lordship of Christ and what that truly means to your life as an overcomer and a Kingdom seeker.

> For this reason also, God highly exalted Him, and bestowed on Him the name which is above every name, so that at the name of Jesus every knee will bow, of those who are in heaven and on earth and under the earth, and that every tongue will confess that Jesus Christ is Lord, to the glory of God the Father.

> — PHILIPPIANS 2:9-11

JUNE 17

"You are holy"

We worship God in His holiness, for His holiness. From our perspective, God is perfect and spotless, without sin. Holy. From His perspective, we who are redeemed by the blood of Christ are pure and holy—set apart for Kingdom work. Just as He is set apart as the God of the Universe, we—as His born again children—are set apart to do the work of ministry. As we pursue our identity in Christ, we must logically come to the conclusion that our identity is one born of holiness, that we are called to be holy, called to live as ones set apart from the world.

Today, let us practice being holy by simply walking in and thinking from our identity in Christ. In so doing, we will be proclaiming by thought, attitude, and action the holiness of God. Worship Him in His holiness by walking as one who knows who and whose they are!

> As obedient children, do not be conformed to the former lusts which were yours in your ignorance, but like the Holy One who called you, be holy yourselves also in all your behavior; because it is written, "You shall be holy, for I am holy."
>
> — 1 PETER 1:14-16

~

JUNE 18

"Holy! Holy! You are Lord"

Sometimes it is good to worship God simply for who He is —regardless of what you perceive He has done or not done for you! When you acknowledge God as *the* Holy One, *the* Lord, *the* Author and Finisher of your faith, *the* Redeemer, *the* center of your very being and identity, you build a highway of intimacy right into His heart!

Why not spend a good part of today's mental energy focusing on who God is in your life and worship Him for being who He is to you? You will find yourself cleansed and encouraged in the process, and God glorified in all your ways!

> Ascribe to the Lord the glory due His name;
> Bring an offering, and come before Him;
> Worship the Lord in holy array.

> — 1 CHRONICLES 16:29

~

JUNE 19

"God and King"

We have come to know who God is—whether we realize it or not—by the meanings of the names He calls Himself. We call Him our *Shepherd* and He guides us. We call Him *Redeemer* because of all He has done to take back the stolen ground in our lives. We call Him *Savior* for literally saving us from sin and Hell. We call Him *Victor* because He has delivered us and brought victory to our once-defeated lives. We call Him *God* because He is the object of our worship. We call Him *King* because He rules and reigns over sin and darkness. We call Him what He calls Himself.

Let us order today by beginning and ending—and filling the time between!—with a ready awareness and acknowledgement of who He is in our lives. Allow Him to sit on the throne of your heart. Call out His name according to your need today and according to the glory due His name!

The name of the Lord is a strong tower;
　　The righteous runs into it and is safe.

— PROVERBS 18:10

~

JUNE 20

"Jesus, my Lord"

In corporate worship, we often say "Jesus is Lord," and this is good. But today, let's take that truth a little deeper by saying "Jesus is *my* Lord." As you meditate on this thought, allow the Holy Spirit to take you to places in your mind of darkness, pain, worry, or fear which would benefit from allowing Jesus access to and lordship over them. When He is Lord over darkness, light is the result. When He is Lord over pain, comfort is the result. When He is Lord over worry, peace is the result. When He is Lord over fear, confidence is the result.

Allow the Lord to build your faith today by simply acknowledging the personal Lordship of Jesus in every area of your life.

God is faithful, through whom you were called into fellowship with His Son, Jesus Christ our Lord.

— 1 CORINTHIANS 1:9

JUNE 21

"God, You are holy"

Let's make today a day of worshiping God for who He is and exalting Him for all He has done to redeem us from the darkness of sin. If He is God, He rules over all. If He is Holy, He is perfect in all His ways. What do those two truths mean to your life? If you are facing hard circumstances, what is His perspective? If you are feeling unloved or alone, what is His reality for you?

Worship God today and simply acknowledge all He has done, and watch the truth of His faithfulness affect your present circumstances. Today, watch victory and joy unfold before you like light piercing the darkness.

> Exalt the Lord our God
>> And worship at His holy hill,
>> For holy is the Lord our God.

— PSALM 99:9

JUNE 22

"Holy! Holy! You are Lord"

Let us focus our minds and hearts on the name of Jesus. What does the name *Jesus* mean? *Jesus* literally means "Jehovah is Salvation" or "God is Salvation." What does the salvation of God mean to you personally? What has it meant to you in your past? What do you need it to mean in your present circumstances? What does the name of Jesus mean to you concerning your future?

Meditate today on the name of Jesus and allow the things the Spirit reveals to filter through every thought, attitude, and action.

> Therefore, having been justified by faith, we have peace with God through our Lord Jesus Christ.

> — ROMANS 5:1

JUNE 23

"Holy! Holy! Holy!"

God is not like us. He is perfect. Perfect in love. Perfect in power. Perfect in nature. Yet, we are created in His likeness, created in His image, created for fellowship with Him. The only way this was possible was through the sacrifice of Jesus Christ, effectively bridging the gap sin made between us and the Father.

Today, let us celebrate His holiness by walking in our identity as sons and daughters of God who are restored to right standing with Father by virtue of the blood of Jesus Christ. Be like Him — be who you truly are in Christ!

> He made Him who knew no sin to be sin on our behalf, so that we might become the righteousness of God in Him.

> — 2 CORINTHIANS 5:21

JUNE 24

"Holy God!"

There is no other like our God—no person, no entity, nothing and no one like Him! There is no hope apart from Him. We can hope in our talents, our looks, our money, our fame, our whatever, yet all of those things fade and fail at some point. We must place our faith and our hope in a perfect God.

Today, let us practice placing hope in our perfect God by simply walking in the reality of who we are because of who He is.

> Exalt the Lord our God
>   And worship at His holy hill,
>   For holy is the Lord our God.

— PSALM 99:9

JUNE 25

"I give You praise for You are holy!"

It is one thing to think good thoughts and say good things *about* the Lord. It is quite another to think and say good things *to* the Lord! In reality, God does not *need* our praise, but He does desire *relationship* with us! Praising God is one of the best ways to practice our relationship with God. To praise God is to thank Him for who He is, for what He has done, and for what He *will* do! Praise sets our minds on the path of righteousness and holiness. Praise puts the enemy under our feet and give no place for his lies to grow. Praise permeates our entire being and fills us with hope, because our God inhabits the praise of His people!

Be inhabited today! Praise God!

Yet You are holy,
O You who are enthroned upon the praises of Israel.

— PSALM 22:3

~

JUNE 26

"When the storms begin to blow"

Listen to the song "In The Shadow Of Thy Wings" from the album *We Are The Army.*

When the storms begin to blow
There is one place that I know that I can go
And I go running there and my heart sings.

When the days grow long and dry
When the enemy would lie to You I cry
As I go running there beneath the shadow of Thy holy wings!

In the shadow of Thy wings!
In the shadow of Thy wings!
I will hide in You!

I will hide in You!
Beneath the shadow of Thy wings!
In the shadow of Thy wings!
In the shadow of Thy wings!
I will hide in You!
I will hide in You!
In You!

In the glory of the King!
Lord, my heart can't help but sing!
I will rest in You, my King!
I will worship You, King!
Beneath the shadow of Thy wings!
In the glory of the King!
Lord, my heart can't help but sing!
I will rest in You, my King!
I will worship You, my King!
My King!

Sin sees to it that life is not easy. As long as we live in this world—until Jesus returns—there will be trials and tribulations, storms and fiery ordeals, sorrow and despair, yet we are a people of hope! When we have no hope, our souls grow sick. When we walk in sickness, we have little strength and no vitality. That is no way to live! We are Children of the Light meant to live *abundantly*! Where is our hope in the stormy, fiery, trials of life? There is only one place—the Solid Rock of Jesus Christ.

Let us see what He sees today. When the storms rage, look beyond and see what He sees. When the fires blaze, see that you are not alone in the midst of the flames. You have hope— He is right there with you!

Hope deferred makes the heart sick,
But desire fulfilled is a tree of life.

— PROVERBS 13:12

~

JUNE 27

"There is one place that I know that I can go"

When all else fails, there is Jesus. When money runs out, there is Jesus. When nothing seems to be going your way, there is Jesus. There is only one constant in life. All else fails and pales in comparison to what and who we have in Jesus. He is our life. He is our joy. He is our Redeemer. He is our Savior. He is our Healer. He is our Shepherd. He is our everything.

Today, let us focus on what it means to allow Jesus to permeate our entire being and existence. Give Him a place at the table of your life and make Him feel welcome. He is where we belong.

When all things are subjected to Him, then the Son Himself also will be subjected to the One who subjected all things to Him, so that God may be all in all.

— 1 CORINTHIANS 15:28

"And I go running there and my heart sings"

Why do we wait until things get really bad before finally submitting to the life and grace and presence of God? It may be that we walk in more self-reliance than we'd like to admit. It may mean that we cower in fear more than we'd like to believe. It may mean that we believe more lies of the enemy than we'd care to consider admitting. Regardless, we must learn to be quick to admit our need for our Savior—no matter how mature or wise we may grow in our faith.

We live in a fallen world that is in need of a Savior. Let us live as people of the Kingdom, knowing our very real need for the very real Savior, and, by our existence, testify to His power as one who walks knowing their need of the Savior.

Therefore do not be ashamed of the testimony of our Lord or of me His prisoner, but join with me in suffering for the gospel according to the power of God, who has saved us and called us with a holy calling, not according to our works, but according to His own purpose and grace which was granted us in Christ Jesus from all eternity, but now has been revealed by the appearing of our Savior Christ Jesus, who abolished death and brought life and immortality to light through the gospel,

— 2 TIMOTHY 1:8-10

~

JUNE 29

"When the days grow long and dry"

Wallowing in worry does not accomplish much. I recently heard it said that worry is a lot like sitting in a rocking chair— you fill a lot of time, but it gets you nowhere. Worry accomplishes nothing. When faced with worry, we must be quick to turn those concerns to the Lord in prayer. Once we have laid our requests out, we must leave them in His strong, able hands and go on with life. We can change nothing by constantly allowing it to fill our minds. When money is short, tell God, trust Him, and live your life without fearing what you don't have. Count your blessings. Do not allow past failures or the consequences of sin to dictate your life. You cannot change the past. Why worry about it anymore? You cannot alter the consequences. Own them. Live them out in grace and move on to what the Lord has in store for you. You may be in a desert, but the Lord is an oasis in its midst.

Today, instead of wallowing in fear of what might be or what could have been, enjoy your life. Live with Jesus *now*.

We are destroying speculations and every lofty thing raised up against the knowledge of God, and we are taking every thought captive to the obedience of Christ.

— 2 CORINTHIANS 10:5

JUNE 30

"When the enemy would lie to you I cry"

We know the enemy of God, Satan, is a liar. We *know* that, yet how often do we succumb to his lying ways? Far too often. As we walk in intimacy with the Lord, we become more attuned to His way of thinking—right thinking—and more aware of the subtleties of the enemy's lies—stinkin' thinkin'. Regardless of what happens, God wants nothing but our best. Regardless of what others think of us and regardless of our failures, we are still God's children!

As we go about our business today, let us think right thoughts about the Lord and ourselves. When a lie is revealed, be quick to cry out to God. Put the lie down, put on the truth, repent if necessary, and move on in God's presence!

> Do not lie to one another, since you laid aside the old self with its evil practices, and have put on the new self who is being renewed to a true knowledge according to the image of the One who created him—a renewal…
>
> — COLOSSIANS 3:9-11A

JUNE 31

"And I go running there"

There is no shame in running from sin, in running from even the suggestion or the appearance of evil. It is the wise believer who runs *to* the battle and takes the enemy head on, defeating him with the Word of God, conquering him with the power of our testimony of deliverance, and not fearing even death itself. When faced with sin or the enemy, the first place we should always run is right into the presence of God. Sometimes, we forget that He's with us, or we try to handle matters on our own, but God never leaves us or forsakes us.

Today, let us utilize the relationship He has given us with Himself and run to the sanctuary of His presence, even in the heat of battle, even in the onslaught of temptation.

> The name of the Lord is a strong tower;
> The righteous runs into it and is safe.
>
> — PROVERBS 18:10

JULY

JULY 1

"Beneath the shadow of Thy holy wings"

The Lord compares Himself to a mother hen who uses her wings to shield her chicks from the sun and from the fangs of those who would harm them. He also compares His reach to the rays of the sun that pierce through the clouds and bring light to darkness. God's presence is like that for us as His children.

When the enemy's lies beset us today, let us be quick to take refuge in the shadow of His wings. Let us be quick to remember that no matter how dark life can become, He is always there shining through. Let us bask in the rays of His presence today.

Keep me as the apple of the eye;

Hide me in the shadow of Your wings
From the wicked who despoil me,
My deadly enemies who surround me.

— PSALM 17:8-9

JULY 2

"In the shadow of Thy wings!"

When I was a boy, we always had geese on our farm. In the springtime, when the new goslings hatched, the mother goose would keep her babies very near. And when she felt a threat — like a dog or a curious boy trying to pick up one of her babies — she would fly into a rage and nip at the dog or the fleeing boy! She was relentless! In sheer panic, the dog (or boy) would run in the opposite direction, having forgotten about the goslings because of the pain being inflicted by the snapping beak of a very irate mother goose! God's fury and jealousy for His children is even more intense than that of the mother protecting her babies.

Rest in that love and protection today. Rely on it.

Be gracious to me, O God, be gracious to me,
    For my soul takes refuge in You;
    And in the shadow of Your wings I will take refuge
    Until destruction passes by.

— PSALM 57:1

JULY 3

"In the shadow of Thy wings!"

God's love for us is faithful, always there just as He is always there. Even when we are distracted by life — even when we forget He is there — our God is still watching over us, brooding over us like a protective hen guarding her chicks. His love is fierce and jealous. He is passionate in His love and righteously irate toward the Enemy who would harm us.

Let us not forget nor allow ourselves to be distracted today. Let us walk as those who know Someone has their back, regardless of trials, tribulations, or circumstances of any kind.

> When I remember You on my bed,
> I meditate on You in the night watches,
> For You have been my help,
> And in the shadow of Your wings I sing for joy.

— PSALM 63:6-7

JULY 4

"I will hide in You!"

It is one thing to hide *from* God and quite another to hide *in* God! It is quite arrogant for us feeble humans to think we can ever hide *anything* from God. He sees the hidden things and loves us anyway! It is equally arrogant to think we can tough life out on our own, facing trials and tribulations without needing God or others. A new creation knows that his or her very existence begins and ends with their reliance upon the presence and grace of God. His presence means we are *never* alone. His grace means we have power to make it through *anything*.

Let us practice the presence of God today and cry out to Him for grace as needed. We will gain an abundance of life through the relationship fostered by such humility.

> Deliver me, O Lord, from my enemies;
> I take refuge in You.

> — PSALM 143:9

JULY 5

"I will hide in You!"

When we are children, we love to play games like hide-and-seek. As an adult who longs to know intimacy with the Lord, I have changed the name to seek-and-hide! I seek Jesus daily and, when I find Him, I like to hide myself in Him. In our sinful state, we used to hide from God rather than seek Him, but in our redeemed state, we seek Him and desire to hide *in* Him. In Him, the cares of the day cannot touch our core identity. Circumstances change but, hidden in Him, we remain constant in attitude because of the constancy of His presence.

Today, let us seek God in attitude, and then, once we sense His work and presence in our life, hide ourselves away in Him. As you live with this attitude, life will abound from every circumstance, and even the pain and sorrow of life become opportunities to practice His presence and minister to others.

> Your adornment must not be merely external — braiding the hair, and wearing gold jewelry, or putting on dresses; but let it be the hidden person of the heart, with the imperishable quality of a gentle and quiet spirit, which is precious in the sight of God.
>
> — 1 PETER 3:3-4

∼

JULY 6

"Beneath the shadow of Thy wings!"

Like a blazing hot sunny day, life can often seem unbearable. But even on the hottest of days, when a solitary cloud passes overhead, for a few brief seconds, we experience a drop in temperature and a psychological lifting due to the shade that little cloud has provided. In the presence of God, we have access to constant "shade" from the heat of life as we simply acknowledge that we are not alone — that He is *with us*.

As you go about your day today, simply take every opportunity afforded you to acknowledge that you are not alone. When you are angry, remember you have One who is with you who understands your frustration. When you are disregarded in some way, remember the One is with you is glad for your existence and never disregards you. Acknowledge God and you will see your life from His point of view, and the grace to overcome will abound.

> The Lord looks from heaven;
>> He sees all the sons of men;
>> From His dwelling place He looks out
>> On all the inhabitants of the earth,
>> He who fashions the hearts of them all,
>> He who understands all their works.

— PSALM 33:13-15

JULY 7

"In the glory of the King!"

The glory of King Jesus is far too massive for the human mind to fully comprehend, but we can try! The glory of God is the actual weight of His presence. I like to think of the weight of His presence in tangible terms I can understand. I like to feel the weight of His love for me much in the way a child likes to feel the weight of a grandmother's arms wrapped around them in sheer joy. I like to feel the weight of His massive redeeming love in the way one who is covered with the day's dusty grime feels when finally able to be cleansed by a long, hot shower.

As you go about the day today, ask the Holy Spirit to allow you to see glimpses of the King's glory in ways that are easy to conceive and difficult to forget. Your faith will be bolstered and your heart made lighter in the process.

Who is the King of glory?
The Lord strong and mighty,
The Lord mighty in battle.
Lift up your heads, O gates,
And lift them up, O ancient doors,
That the King of glory may come in!

— PSALM 24:8-9

JULY 8

"Lord, my heart can't help but sing!"

Do you remember times as a child when the sheer joy of being alive caused you to sing or whistle or skip around? I do, but life has a way—sin has a way—of causing us to lose that joy. In Christ, as new creations, we are freed from the chains of sin and freed from the guilt of our past failures. So why do we lapse back into feelings of worthlessness or shame and guilt? We simply forget who we are and whose we are. When we do that the enemy floods in with his lies that try to cause us to focus on everything but God's perspective.

Today, let us remember to be aware of the Liar's schemes and be ready to put down his lies and put on the truth. The truth? To see what God sees, and watch the joy flood back in, watch the skip in your step return, and watch the song in your heart resound!

Restore to me the joy of Your salvation
And sustain me with a willing spirit.

— PSALM 51:12

JULY 9

"I will rest in You, my King!"

Jesus promises rest for our souls if we simply come to Him with open hearts. Honest confession—of hurts, wounds, failures, or stinkin' thinkin'—always has the effect of making us aware of how self-focused we have become and how much we need the Lord's presence in our lives!

Let us rest in the King today. If you are tired of being hurt, rest in and allow His healing to rule and reign in your life, and do not fear the risk of rejection love requires. If you are tired of how easily it seems you succumb to the enemy's lies, rest in and allow the truth of the King's acceptance of you to rule and reign in your heart and mind. Rest in the fact that you are a servant of the King of all Kings!

> Come to Me, all who are weary and heavy-laden, and I will give you rest. Take My yoke upon you and learn from Me, for I am gentle and humble in heart, and you will find rest for your souls. For My yoke is easy and My burden is light.
>
> — MATTHEW 11:28-30

JULY 10

"I will worship You, my King!"

Worship is intimate communion with God. We can all stand a little intimacy in our lives, right? Intimacy is the very key to life. On a physical level, the human race would not continue without it! On a spiritual level, the human race cannot survive or have real meaning without it!

Today, let us focus on worshiping God in every sense of the word. Worship Him in songs of praise. Worship Him in attitude. Worship Him in service to others. Worship Him in thought and deed. Just simply acknowledge His presence and allow Him to acknowledge *yours*.

> Then the King will desire your beauty.
> Because He is your Lord, bow down to Him.

> — PSALM 45:11

JULY 11

"Beneath the shadow of Thy wings!"

Like a mighty oak that brings shade to all who come under its expansive branches, the presence of our God is a place of refuge for the new creation. If you have financial needs, acknowledge His presence as your provider and rest in the shadow of His provision. If you have need for physical healing today, acknowledge His presence as your Healer and find rest in His healing presence. If you have need of intimacy— someone who simply understands you—find rest in the shadow of His constant presence in your life and pour out your heart to Him in that place. All that we need in this life is found beneath the shadow of His expansive reach.

Rest in His presence today and find sustaining power for the life you are called to live.

How precious is Your lovingkindness, O God!

And the children of men take refuge in the shadow of Your wings.

— PSALM 36:7

JULY 12

"I will rest in You, my King!"

Sometimes, we forget to rest. Sometimes, we really have no time to rest. Sometimes, the times we set aside to rest get interrupted by pressing needs. You know the routine. God has ordained that we take a rest—a Sabbath—from our labors once a week. There is wisdom in that and health for our soul and body. But what do we do when that is not anywhere near our reality? We must learn to rest in creative ways!

Today, during the busyness of your day, ask the Lord to give you insight into creative ways to grab a few minutes of rest with Him, when you can download your thoughts onto His broad shoulders and allow Him to carry the burden for you. Remember to see from *His* perspective.

Take My yoke upon you and learn from Me, for I am gentle and humble in heart, and you will find rest for your souls. For My yoke is easy and My burden is light.

— MATTHEW 11:29

"I trust in Thee like a child and Father"

Listen to the song "I Trust In Thee" from the album *We Are The Army.*

I trust in Thee like a child and Father
Lord, I trust in Thee!
With my heart I trust in Thee!

I trust in Thee like a servant to His King!
I trust in Thee!
With my heart I trust in Thee!

You want my hands?
Lord, here they are!
You want my soul?
Then take my heart!
You want my trust?
To You I call!
You want my life?
Lord, take it all!

A child grows up—ideally—learning trust by trusting his or her parents. But sin and the world have a way of shattering trust. Anger. Abuse. Apathy. Lying. Broken promises. Many things can lead a child to a place where trust is broken. Even if we had great earthly fathers, they are still less than perfect. Our heavenly Father *is* perfect, and we can trust Him in that perfection. So let's remember to not see Father through the filter of our earthly father but to see Him for who He is.

Regardless of what our personal issues are, we all need a place to let our guard down—a place where we can put our hearts on display, with assurance they will be handled with great tender, loving care. Let us practice trusting our heavenly Father today by putting our hearts out there for Him. Whatever your need, entrust it to Him.

Just as a father has compassion on his children,
So the Lord has compassion on those who fear Him.

— PSALM 103:13

JULY 14

"Lord, I Trust in Thee"

To trust God is to have confidence in His abilities. To have confidence in His abilities requires faith on our part. To walk in faith requires that we believe He only desires our best—even when He allows hard or harsh times in our existence. If we can learn to see Father and His ways from *His* point of view, rather than from our sin-skewed point of view, we will see a bigger picture of His capacity—to waste nothing in our lives when we offer those things to Him in honest confession.

Do you trust Jesus today? Do you have confidence in Him and His ways? Ask the Holy Spirit to let you see what He sees, and watch trust grow.

But let all who take refuge in You be glad,

Let them ever sing for joy;
And may You shelter them,
That those who love Your name may exult in You.

— PSALM 5:11

JULY 15

"With my heart I trust in Thee I trust in Thee"

My heart is the very core of my existence. I am not speaking of my physical heart but, rather, the essence of who I am. As a living being, it is innate to fight for every breath. That is the way we were designed—to maintain our existence on this planet. But we were designed to fight for our spiritual existence as well. Every person is born with a deep, innate need to seek God. Sin muddies the path and leads us down far too many dead ends, leaves us shattered in wreckage at times. This tends to ruin our trust. But if we truly desire a deeper life—a richer, fuller life—we must seek the very Source of that life, by seeking our Creator.

Today, trust your hurts and any failures to Him. He can handle it. He is the Author of Life. Trust your heart to Him deeply today.

I will give thanks to the Lord with all my heart;
I will tell of all Your wonders.

— PSALM 9:1

JULY 16

"Like a servant to his King I trust in Thee"

To serve another is, in a sense, to lay down your life for the one you serve. To serve requires humility—seeing the one you serve as more important than yourself. What is so wonderful about serving Jesus is that He first served us by laying down His life for us. And to make matters even more incredible, He turns around and offers us grace—the power and desire—to serve Him!

We serve a great King. We serve One who has led and taught us by example. Let us honor our King today by serving those He would serve. Let us serve in humility of attitude, in humility of thought, in humility of word, in humility of action. Let us see all we think or do as acts of service to our King. It will revolutionize our very lives.

But the greatest among you shall be your servant.

— MATTHEW 23:11

JULY 17

"With my heart I trust in Thee"

Trust is confidence in something or someone. It can also be defined as reliance on something or someone. To rely on Jesus means we believe He is who He says He is and that He will do what He says He will do. To rely on Jesus is to believe He loves us and that He desires only what is good for us. I rely on my vehicle to get me places, but sometimes that vehicle lets me down and leaves me stranded! Jesus has never once left me stranded—even when it *felt* like He had! My point? Jesus uses *everything* in our lives to bring about a greater awareness of our true identity in Him. He wastes nothing.

Feeling stranded today? Look around. Jesus is up to only good! See what He sees and rely on Him there.

> Guard my soul and deliver me;
> Do not let me be ashamed, for I take refuge in You.
>
> — PSALM 25:20

JULY 18

"You want my hands? Lord, here they are"

We sing songs declaring that we "surrender" to the Lord, yet we walk away surrendering only portions of our existence, surrendering only what we feel comfortable giving up. To *surrender* is to relinquish control of something to someone else. We want to lose weight, yet we are not willing to surrender the control of our appetite. We want financial freedom, yet we are not willing to surrender control of our desire to spend more than we have. We want friends, yet we are not willing to surrender our comfort and go out and meet people. Why do we do that? Because we want to maintain control of our destinies. Because we are afraid of being hurt. Because we care more about instant gratification than long-term success. If we relinquish control, who is there to keep us safe? But if we lose control by surrendering our needs to Christ, we will actually be gaining life in the process.

Think about this today and see what the Holy Spirit reveals to you. Step out in faith and trust Him in whatever area He leads you.

> He who has found his life will lose it, and he who has lost his life for My sake will find it.
>
> — MATTHEW 10:39

~

JULY 19

"You want my soul? Then take my heart"

When we are children, we abandon ourselves in play. Even during times of heartache, as a child, I was still able to find joy when I simply enjoyed *being*. I remember my dad taking me by both hands and swinging me around and around, lifting me higher and higher with each turn. That was a *dangerous* thing from a child's perspective, but because I trusted my dad to keep hold of me, I *enjoyed* the ride! In a sense, my dad had me by the heart—by the core of my being—and I trusted him completely. That is how I want to live with my heavenly Father —trusting Him completely and enjoying the ride—no matter the danger involved! Loving others means risking rejection, but to not risk rejection is to not enjoy life.

Live dangerously today. Love God. Trust God. Love others. And trust Him to hang on to you as He lifts you higher and higher!

> But as for me, the nearness of God is my good;
>> I have made the Lord God my refuge,
>> That I may tell of all Your works.

— PSALM 73:28

~

JULY 20

"You want my trust? To You I call"

Let's practice what we preach today. Let's carry on a constant dialog with the Lord that is very intentional. Whether we feel His presence or not—and whether we are angry, sad, or completely apathetic—let's call out to the Lord. When you drive to work, ask Him questions. When you have conflict with someone, ask God how to deal with that conflict in love. If someone hurts you, take that burden instantly to the Lord and respond accordingly. In each circumstance, cry out to the Lord and listen for His response. In so doing, we will practice placing our trust completely in Him and will deepen our intimacy with Him. The benefits are too numerous to list.

Let's trust God today by simply talking with Him.

I call upon the Lord, who is worthy to be praised,
And I am saved from my enemies.

— PSALM 18:3

JULY 21

"You want my life? Lord, take it all"

What is surrender? To surrender is to relinquish control. Think about this. When we surrender control of our desires in an area of an addiction, we are actually taking control away from the addiction and placing it somewhere else. What was once victorious over us—the addictive attitude—has now been defeated by an act of surrender to God! Surrendering an area of our lives to the Lord is simply responding out of our true identity in Christ. I am His child. As His child, I have been freed from the bondage of sinful thinking and released to a whole new way of thinking about God and about myself. We surrender our identity to Him and are freed from our old ways of thinking. What the enemy wants us to see is what we lost, but what God reveals is a kingdom's worth of possibilities. We surrender one life but gain an eternity's worth!

Meditate on this truth today, and walk in greater freedom according to your identity in Christ as a new creation!

So if the Son makes you free, you will be free indeed.

— JOHN 8:36

JULY 22

"What time I am afraid I will trust in Thee"

Listen to "What Time I Am Afraid" from the album *We Are The Army*.

What time I am afraid
I will trust in Thee!
When I can't see the way
I will trust in Thee!
What time I need a friend
I will trust in Thee!
SomeOne to hold my hand
I will trust in Thee!
Jesus! Jesus! Jesus! Jesus!
What time I am afraid
I will trust in Thee!
When I can't see the way
I will trust in Thee!

What causes us to fear? Loss? Pain? A lack of trust? If we do not trust that someone will return our love, we fear relationships. If we fear someone or something will cause us pain or harm, we fear for our own safety. Fear can be a good thing when it preserves our lives or mental and emotional well-being. But irrational fear—that God is not in control—reduces us to relying on our own strength and ability or causes to placing our trust in another.

Today, allow the Holy Spirit to reveal irrational as well as healthy fear. Fear of heights or sharks? Healthy fear. Fear that

God will not meet our needs? Irrational. Think about it. Release the irrational and trust God with the reality of His presence. As for the healthy fears? Trust God there as well!

When I am afraid, I will put my trust in You.

— PSALM 56:3

JULY 23

"When I can't see the way I will trust in Thee"

What do we do when our homes suddenly loses power on a stormy night? We immediately search for a flashlight or a match to light a candle. What do we do when we suddenly lose the light of direction during a spiritual storm of life? Far too often, we try to light our own way with worldly wisdom and personal strength. We wind up stumbling around in the dark and hurting ourselves! In times of spiritual darkness, it is best to reach for the light of Jesus Christ. When we need wisdom or comfort or direction, we need look only as far as our own hearts, where the glory of God dwells!

Today, if a sudden storm brings a power loss, trust Him. Find His light and find a way out of the darkness!

Light arises in the darkness for the upright;
He is gracious and compassionate and righteous.

— PSALM 112:4

JULY 24

"What time I need a friend I will trust in Thee"

Let's get very personal today. What do you look for in a friend? Someone who understands you. Someone who allows you to air your dirty laundry. Someone who encourages you to be all you can be—to be yourself. Someone to share your life. Someone to scatter loneliness and bring joy in dark times. Someone to share hurts and burdens with. Someone who is there. Someone who has your back. Someone who will love you even when you mess up. People will always let us down. Love keeps on loving even when they do. That is the way of the new creation. And we have One who is our *best* friend.

Spend time meditating on what it means for Jesus to be your friend.

A friend loves at all times.

— PROVERBS 17:17A

JULY 25

"Someone to hold my hand...I will trust in Thee"

When we are small children, a parent holding our hand brings comfort and security and safety. When we are married, our spouse takes us by the hand and evokes romance and intimacy and love and security. There is power holding another's hand. It engenders trust and intimacy. It conveys blessing and identity. People can do that for one another, but God's hand is even more able!

Today, practice holding the hand of God by faith, and practice letting Him hold yours.

My times are in Your hand;
Deliver me from the hand of my enemies and from those who persecute me.

— PSALM 31:15

JULY 26

"Jesus! Jesus! Jesus! Jesus!"

Jesus. When you hear that name, what do you think of? When you say that name, what feelings come to mind? Who is Jesus to you—God, Lord, Savior, Friend?

Today, spend time meditating on who Jesus is to you. Take time to commune with Him in that capacity. In times of worry or fear, call out to Him as Victor. In times of indecision, call out to Him as the Giver of Wisdom. In times of loneliness, call out to Him as Emmanuel—God with you. Meditate on who He is and, more specifically, who He is to *you!*

"Behold, the virgin shall be with child and shall bear a son, and they shall call his name Immanuel," which translated means, "God with us."

— MATTHEW 1:23

"At the name of Jesus every knee will bow"

Listen to "At The Name Of Jesus" from the album *The Dennis Jernigan Collection.*

At the name of Jesus
Ev'ry knee will bow:
He is Lord, He is Lord!

At the name of Jesus
Ev'ry tongue will shout:
He is Lord, He is Lord,
He is Lord, He is Lord!

Blessed is the holy name,
Blessed is the King who reigns,
Blessed is the holy name of Jesus!
Blessed is the holy name,
Blessed is the King who reigns,
Blessed is the holy name of Jesus!
Lord, we praise Your holy name!
Praise Your holy name!

Everyone serves something or someone. Everyone worships something or someone. Who we serve and who we worship directly affects and guides every aspect of our lives. Wisdom is serving and worshiping the King of Kings who is Lord of Lords. Who we serve and worship affects our view of the world, our view of others, and our view of ourselves. Why not fill our minds with all that is good and right and holy? Why not fill our lives with victory and wisdom? Why not serve and worship *the* Victor?

Today, allow the Holy Spirit to show you ways to serve and worship the Lord Jesus Christ that you may not have thought of before, then serve and worship Him in that way.

> So that at the name of Jesus every knee will bow, of those who are in heaven and on earth and under the earth, and that every tongue will confess that Jesus Christ is Lord, to the glory of God the Father.

> — PHILIPPIANS 2:10-11

JULY 28

"He is Lord! He is Lord!"

Jesus is Lord no matter what the world says or does! That is good news! That is *wonderful* news! It means that regardless of what happens, God is in control. It means that regardless of what transpires around us, nothing changes between us and our Lord. It means that nothing changes in the end! Whether we live or die, we will be *with* Him!

Meditate on this Kingdom perspective throughout the day today. Allow the truth of this wisdom to permeate how you view yourself and minister to others.

> God is faithful, through whom you were called into fellowship with His Son, Jesus Christ our Lord.

> — 1 CORINTHIANS 1:9

JULY 29

"At the name of Jesus every tongue will shout"

There is power in the words we speak. With our words, we can speak blessing or we can destroy. Why is that? We are created in the image of our God. He *spoke* everything that exists into existence! His Son, our Savior, is called the *Word* of God! That means that the power to speak is a great responsibility we, as new creations, have been given.

Today, meditate on this truth and allow the Holy Spirit to help you discern the right words to speak in any given situation. Speak blessing and life to others. Speak blessing and life to *yourself!* Speak words of blessing and honor and life *to* the Lord and *about* the Lord, and watch the words you sow reap a harvest of blessing in return.

> Death and life are in the power of the tongue,
>   And those who love it will eat its fruit.
>
> — PROVERBS 18:21

> So that at the name of Jesus every knee will bow, of those who are in heaven and on earth and under the earth, and that every tongue will confess that Jesus Christ is Lord, to the glory of God the Father.
>
> — PHILIPPIANS 2:10-11

"He is Lord! He is Lord! He is Lord! He is Lord!"

As new creations—as those who live according to the view-point of the King—what does it mean when we say Jesus is Lord? Spend time today thinking about the Lordship of Jesus Christ in your life but with this as your viewpoint: how does Jesus being Lord of your life affect the way you treat others? How does it affect the way you think about yourself? How does it affect the way you worship God? How does it affect the way you make decisions? Remember, Jesus is Lord of All, and is full of mercy and grace.

For while I was passing through and examining the objects of your worship, I also found an altar with this inscription, "To an unknown God." Therefore what you worship in ignorance, this I proclaim to you. The God who made the world and all things in it, since He is Lord of heaven and earth, does not dwell in temples made with hands; nor is He served by human hands, as though He needed anything, since He Himself gives to all people life and breath and all things; and He made from one man every nation of mankind to live on all the face of the earth, having determined their appointed times and the boundaries of their habitation, that they would seek God, if perhaps they might grope for Him and find Him, though He is not far from each one of us; for in Him we live and move and exist, as even some of your own poets have said, "For we also are His children."

— ACTS 17:23-28

JULY 31

"Blessed is the holy name!"

Let us spend time today extolling, exalting, and blessing the name of Jesus. When we exalt the Lord, there is freedom. When we exalt the Lord, the enemy is put down. When we exalt and bless the Lord, our soul is infused with life. When we extol the Lord, our attitudes are recalibrated. When we bless His name, God inhabits our very praises! What is the downside to blessing the Lord? There are only positives!

Let us fill our lives with what is good and right and positive this day, and watch our very attitudes come into alignment with all God calls good!

Blessed be the name of the Lord
    From this time forth and forever.
    From the rising of the sun to its setting
    The name of the Lord is to be praised.

— PSALM 113:2-3

AUGUST

AUGUST 1

"Blessed is the King who reigns!"

Isn't it good to know that someone is in control? As children, if we are blessed with caring parents, we find great security and room to grow when our needs are met—when mom and dad are in control! Our God, the King of the Universe, is in control. In His way of thinking—Kingdom thinking—He wastes nothing! He will take even our failures—if we confess them to Him in honesty—and make something beautiful.

Spend time today focused on the fact that God is in control regardless of our circumstances. When we fear, wisdom means asking Him what He sees in that fearful situation. When we are wounded, wisdom means getting to His point of view concerning the wound. Spend time today simply seeing life from His perspective, and respond as a child of the King of the Universe!

> Let the heavens be glad, and let the earth rejoice;
>> And let them say among the nations, "The Lord reigns."

— 1 CHRONICLES 16:31

AUGUST 2

"Blessed is the holy name of Jesus!"

The name of Jesus is used in a variety of ways in our day and time. I cringe whenever I hear someone use His name in vain—to express disgust or as a cuss word. But something I must consider is that the Lord can use even these misuses of His name in a good and holy way. Why do I say that? Because I believe there is power and hope and healing and love in His name—regardless of how it is used! How's that for a Kingdom point of view?

Today, let's determine to use His name as it was intended and to use its misuse as a point of prayer and hope for the person who misused it. In this way, love wins the day!

> Blessed is the one who comes in the name of the Lord;
>> We have blessed you from the house of the Lord.

— PSALM 118:26

AUGUST 3

"Blessed is the holy name!"

The name of Jesus is blessed and holy. If we are His and He has ordained even our given names, let us spend time today meditating on the meanings of our *own* names! Let us embrace our name's meaning and see it from the King's perspective. Let us think of ourselves in regard to our name's meaning. Let us embrace the reality of who our Father says we are. Your name, given by God, is indeed blessed and holy, and so are you!

A good name is to be more desired than great wealth,
 Favor is better than silver and gold.

— PROVERBS 22:1

∼

AUGUST 4

"Blessed is the King who reigns!"

Jesus is the King of Kings. Either He reigns or He doesn't. If He reigns even in circumstances we feel are out of control, then our entire point of view changes, and everything, all we experience, is about the Kingdom of God! We are royal priests of His Kingdom.

If this is the truth, let us rise up and embrace our true identity and destiny, and let it begin by simply acknowledging that, "Today, I will walk as a child of *the* King!"

> But you are a chosen race, a royal priesthood, a holy nation, a people for God's own possession, so that you may proclaim the excellencies of Him who has called you out of darkness into His marvelous light.
>
> — 1 PETER 2:9

AUGUST 5

"Blessed is the holy name of Jesus!"

Let today be consumed with prayer. Let us remember that Jesus is our High Priest—the One who approaches the Father on our behalf. Let your day be consumed with blessing the name of Jesus. With using His name to push back the enemy. In calling out to Him when you need help. In calling out to Him as a friend when you feel alone. In simply communicating your feelings to Him. Unburdening your soul is good, wise, and healing to your entire being.

> But Jesus, on the other hand, because He continues forever, holds His priesthood permanently. Therefore He is able also to save forever those who draw near to God through Him, since He always lives to make intercession for them.
>
> — HEBREWS 7:24-25

AUGUST 6

"Lord, we praise Your holy name!"

Make today a day of simply praising and thanking God for who He is. Here are some reminders about His character. He is your Shepherd. He is your righteousness. He is your Holiness. He is constantly with you. He is your Victory. He is your Healer. He is your Peace. He is Love. He is Father. He is Provider. He is Helper. He is Comforter. He is your All in All. Exalt Him! Thank Him! Bless Him!

I will give thanks to the Lord according to His righteousness
And will sing praise to the name of the Lord Most High.

— PSALM 7:17

AUGUST 7

"Praise Your holy name!"

There is something special about saying the name of a loved one. When you call out to your child, spouse, or dear friend, you don't even have to think about their qualities. The affirmation you feel from them is attached to their name. The affection you feel from them is right there in your heart. The acceptance you feel from the one you call out to is apparent by only saying their name. So it is with the Lord.

Today, spend time saying the names of God throughout the day and see where the Holy Spirit takes you. He is Jesus.

Some of His other names are Emmanuel, Father, Healer, Provider, Peace, Victory, Redeemer, and Friend. Say His name often and allow the Spirit to minister the depth of that name to your soul.

> To You I shall offer a sacrifice of thanksgiving,
> And call upon the name of the Lord.

— PSALM 116:17

AUGUST 8

"I am not my own - I belong to the Lord"

I find great rest and peace in knowing I am no longer my own. In the past, I sat as the king, an all-wise leader of my own life, and my feeble, earthly, human wisdom led me straight down the path of destruction! When the Lord paid my debt, He effectively purchased me—ransomed me—from the grip of my sin and from the lies of the enemy. And the truth of the matter is, *nothing* can separate me from the love of my Father, because all I am belongs to all of Him!

Let that truth soak your soul today!

> For I am persuaded, that neither death, nor life, nor angels, nor principalities, nor powers, nor things present, nor things to come, nor height, nor depth, nor any other creature, shall be able to separate us from the love of God, which is in Christ Jesus our Lord.

— ROMANS 8:38-39

AUGUST 9

"I've been bought with a price I could never afford"

If left to our own devices and wisdom, we will destroy our lives. Thanks be to God that He saw fit to rescue us from sin, and from ourselves! The reality is that sin leaves a debt we can never repay on our own. Money can't buy us out of that debt. Performance and good behavior cannot buy us out of that debt. What others think of us can never pay that debt. There is only One who could ever pay our debt and that is Jesus, and He has paid our debt in *full*! He paid our past debt, our present debt, and our future debt! Hallelujah!

Let this truth permeate your thoughts today. Continue to receive His forgiveness and remember to forgive yourself!

> For you have been bought with a price: therefore glorify God in your body.
>
> — 1 CORINTHIANS 6:20

AUGUST 10

"By the blood of the Lamb Satan's work is undone"

Either the victory afforded us by the blood of Jesus is complete or it is not. The blood of Jesus thoroughly cleanses our sin, completely pays our debt, and provides power over the works of the enemy—power over His lies! We have been completely exonerated by the blood of Jesus, and our victory over the lies of the enemy is equally complete! You and I are victorious, even when circumstances say otherwise, and even when our past failures say otherwise. We are running a race, and we have been given the ultimate victory by the blood of Jesus.

Ponder this today and be the victor the blood of Jesus sealed you to be.

> Knowing that you were not redeemed with perishable things like silver or gold from your futile way of life inherited from your forefathers, but with precious blood, as of a lamb unblemished and spotless, the blood of Christ.
>
> — 1 PETER 1:18-19

AUGUST 11

"I'm a testimony that the blood has overcome"

Have you ever thought of yourself as a testimony to the power of God? If you are a new creation in Christ, that is exactly what you are! If you simply live the love you have been granted by your relationship with God—live out the reality of your exchanged life—others will see and come to desire what you have. They will want to know how you can walk in such grace while experiencing the same hardship and heartache that they are. The best sermons are lived rather than preached.

Live as one who knows who and whose they are today!

> For our proud confidence is this: the testimony of our conscience, that in holiness and godly sincerity, not in fleshly

wisdom but in the grace of God, we have conducted ourselves in the world, and especially toward you.

— 2 CORINTHIANS 1:12

AUGUST 12

"You, Oh God, are a mighty God!"

Let us take time to ponder the might of God in our lives today. Ask yourself these questions to get the meditation going. Where was I twenty years ago in relation to God? Where was I ten years ago? What heartache has the Lord brought me through? What wounds has He healed me of? What evidence of His provision is there in my life? Are there any promises from His Word that have profoundly affected my life? As you ask yourself these questions, allow the Holy Spirit to show you things you may have forgotten or perhaps never even saw, then thank Him!

For a child will be born to us, a son will be given to us;
And the government will rest on His shoulders;
And His name will be called Wonderful Counselor, Mighty God, Eternal Father, Prince of Peace.

— ISAIAH 9:6

AUGUST 13

"You rule, Oh King, with a mighty rod!"

We see Jesus as the King of Kings *and* the Good Shepherd. A king rules with a scepter or rod which denotes his authority. A shepherd uses his rod to protect his sheep. Let us think about King Jesus wielding His rod of authority over the lies of the enemy today. Let us ponder Shepherd Jesus using His rod to protect us from the schemes of the enemy today. As we remind ourselves of the authority of Jesus, it is wise to remember that He has granted us the same power over the deceiver and his deception!

Walk as one under the authority of the King and as one following the Shepherd. Be a mighty servant of the King and a tender sheep of the Shepherd.

> Even though I walk through the valley of the shadow of death,
> I fear no evil, for You are with me;
> Your rod and Your staff, they comfort me.

> — PSALM 23:4

AUGUST 14

"You, Oh God, are invincible!"

When we say something is invincible we are saying that something is literally incapable of being defeated. Our God fits that description, and nothing else! Even the greatest weapons on Earth can be defeated. Even the mightiest armies on Earth can be defeated. Even the strongest person we know will one day succumb to the defeat of old age! It stands to reason that, if we wish to be victorious in life, we should not place our hope in anything but the Lord!

Walk as one who knows the power of their invincible God today, and walk in the power of your true identity as His child!

> He who dwells in the shelter of the Most High
> Will abide in the shadow of the Almighty.
>
> — PSALM 91:1

AUGUST 15

"You, Oh God, undefeatable!"

Our God cannot be defeated. It is an absolute impossibility. So why don't we trust Him when our world is falling apart? My personal belief is that we take our eyes off of the Solution and focus on the circumstances. We must to endure those circumstances regardless, but to see them from our own perspective is one thing, to view them from the King's perspective is another. One causes despair while the other gives hope and assurance.

When faced with the circumstances of life today, choose to get quickly to the Lord's perspective. Do not allow your circumstances—those usurpers of the truth—to dictate your response to life. Live in reality—God's reality!

When the Lord your God brings you into the land where you
are entering to possess it, and clears away many nations
before you, the Hittites and the Girgashites and the Amorites
and the Canaanites and the Perizzites and the Hivites and
the Jebusites, seven nations greater and stronger than
you, and when the Lord your God delivers them before you
and you defeat them, then you shall utterly destroy them.
You shall make no covenant with them and show no favor to
them.

— DEUTERONOMY 7:1-2

AUGUST 16

"You can cast a mountain to the sea!"

Sometimes it is easier for us to believe God can move a
literal mountain than it is to believe He can move the mountain
of our earthly perspective which keeps us from seeing Him. It
is when we can see only the storm that we forget the harbor of
His presence. It is in the fiery furnace of circumstance that we
forget He is right there with us in the midst of the trial,
burning away all that in not necessary for an abundant life.

Today, let us allow Him to move the mountains of our
earthly perspective, and let us find victory in seeing from His
vantage point.

Truly I say to you, whoever says to this mountain, "Be taken
up and cast into the sea," and does not doubt in his heart, but
believes that what he says is going to happen, it will be
granted him. Therefore I say to you, all things for which you

pray and ask, believe that you have received them, and they will be granted you.

— MARK 11:23-24

AUGUST 17

"You can overcome the enemy!"

At times it feels like we will be overcome and overrun by the lies of the enemy. When those times occur, it serves us well to remember who we are and whose we are. We are new creations, sons and daughters, of the Most High God. We have been bought with a price and redeemed by a Jealous God who does not take kindly to the Enemy messing with His children!

Today, let us walk in the belief of who we are as we purpose to think like new creations. Today, let us walk in assurance of victory as we purpose to walk like those who know their God is extremely jealous for them!

For the Lord your God is a consuming fire, a jealous God.

— DEUTERONOMY 4:24

AUGUST 18

"You can overflow the heart of me!"

Do you remember how empty you felt when you were consumed by sin? Do you remember how numb you felt when you went through times of so much pain you didn't even care anymore, thinking "what does one more hurt matter?" After we are born again and begin to unburden our souls to the Lord, His love flows in those places of honest confession, and we are able to feel again where we had grown hard and numb and callous. We can have that overflow each and every day as we seek Jesus in intimacy.

Ask the Holy Spirit to fill you to overflowing today with whatever you need!

> That He would grant you, according to the riches of His glory, to be strengthened with power through His Spirit in the inner man, so that Christ may dwell in your hearts through faith; and that you, being rooted and grounded in love, may be able to comprehend with all the saints what is the breadth and length and height and depth, and to know the love of Christ which surpasses knowledge, that you may be filled up to all the fullness of God.
>
> — EPHESIANS 3:16-19

AUGUST 19

"For You are reigning King!"

So many times the Enemy is able to get us to a point where it feels and seems like evil is winning the day. It is in those times that we must remember the end of the story, and we must remember to see even those evil moments as a part of the bigger picture. The reality of that big picture? Jesus wins. We win. Even if we experience the worst-case scenario—we die—we still win! Whether we live or whether we die, we will be with Jesus!

Today, let us remember to step back from our circumstances and ask the Holy Spirit to give us the Kingdom point of view—to see the big picture of just how victorious He is and we are!

> For this reason also, God highly exalted Him, and bestowed on Him the name which is above every name, so that at the name of Jesus every knee will bow, of those who are in heaven and on earth and under the earth, and that every tongue will confess that Jesus Christ is Lord, to the glory of God the Father.
>
> — PHILIPPIANS 2:9-11

~

AUGUST 20

"You, Oh God, are a mighty God!"

God is the strength of our life. This means that God is all-powerful even when we are at our weakest. The joy of the Lord is our strength. This means we know who we are and whose we are regardless of our situation or circumstance, and we are learning to walk more and more in the reality of this truth. Our God never fails. Even when bad things happen, we are not alone and He is still good, wanting only what is best for us.

Let us cling to these truths today and keep the Enemy under our feet where he belongs! Our God *is* mighty!

Behold, God is mighty but does not despise any;
    He is mighty in strength of understanding.

— JOB 36:5

AUGUST 21

"You rule, Oh King, with a mighty rod!"

We have already established that our God is a Good Shepherd—leading, guiding, and protecting with His Shepherd's rod—and the King of Kings—ruling and reigning over our lives by the authority of His royalty. If He is our Shepherd, we are His sheep.

What green pastures and fresh waters do you need today? Be honest with the Lord about your needs. You have not, because you ask not. If He is our King, then He rules over the realm of our life and desires victory for His subjects. Be honest with the Lord and tell Him the battles you face today. Be looking for the feast set before you in the midst of your Enemy, and sit down and partake!

You prepare a table before me in the presence of my enemies.

— PSALM 23:5A

AUGUST 22

"You, Oh God, are invincible!"

Are there any areas of your life where you feel defeated today? Are there any areas where you feel overwhelmed? Have you confessed these areas to God in honesty? It is when we empty our hearts in honest, intimate confession that our God is able to take our emptiness and fill it with His presence and perspective. Wisdom is simply seeing each situation from God's perspective, but we never gain that perspective if we do not fellowship with Him.

Empty your heart in honesty to Him, then open that empty place to receive what He pours in!

I know how to get along with humble means, and I also know how to live in prosperity; in any and every circumstance I have learned the secret of being filled and going hungry, both of having abundance and suffering need.

— PHILIPPIANS 4:12

AUGUST 23

"You, Oh God, undefeatable!"

We all go through times when we feel defeated. Sometimes we are defeated by our own failure. Sometimes we are defeated when let down by someone else. Sometimes we feel defeated when our plans fall through or a dream is crushed. There are simply many ways defeated-ness can wend its way into our minds. What is the Kingdom truth? Even when defeat comes, King Jesus wins! Since we are children of the Kingdom, we win when we learn to see each and every situation and circumstance from the King's point of view.

Spend time reminding your own soul to do this today and walk in freedom!

> The LORD your God is in your midst,
>> A victorious warrior.
>> He will exult over you with joy,
>> He will be quiet in His love,
>> He will rejoice over you with shouts of joy.

> — ZEPHANIAH 3:17

AUGUST 24

"For You are a mighty God!"

We often worship God by extolling His might. Today, let's be very specific. Make a list of all the times God has shown up in your life in a mighty way. If you have trouble thinking of anything, spend time asking the Lord to prove Himself mighty in a specific circumstance you are currently facing, then step back and watch what He does. Be patient and remember to take God out of the box of your limitations, because when we place Him in a box, that is all we get of Him. Allow the Spirit to guide you to see His mighty hand in ways you may have overlooked.

> O Lord God of hosts, who is like You, O mighty Lord?
> Your faithfulness also surrounds You.

— PSALM 89:8

~

AUGUST 25

"We're a holy nation"

Believer, when is the last time you reminded yourself of who you are in Christ? Let us do that very thing today. When we define ourselves by our temptations, we see confusion in the mirror. When we define ourselves by our failures, we see only despair in the mirror. When we define ourselves by our past, we see disgust in the mirror. Why would we ever define ourselves in any way other than how our Father defines us? When we define ourselves as redeemed, we see purity in the mirror. When we define ourselves as new creations, we see hope and a future in the mirror. When we define ourselves as sons and daughters of Almighty God, we see a victorious warrior in the mirror. When we define ourselves in the way Father defines us, we see Jesus! How do you see yourself today? Be who *Father* says you are.

> But you are a chosen race, a royal priesthood, a holy nation,
> a people for God's own possession, so that you may proclaim

the excellencies of Him who has called you out of darkness
into His marvelous light.

— 1 PETER 2:9

AUGUST 26

"We're the army of the Lord"

Doesn't it feel good to belong to a group? When sides are being selected for games, we long to be chosen. And we often face disappointment when chosen last—or not chosen at all! There is great news, though. We, in Christ, never have to worry about being chosen again! We have been chosen—wanted and adopted—by Father Himself! We *do* belong! Whether we realize it or not, once we are in Christ we become a part of a holy army of believers called the body of Christ! We need to not take that lightly! We need to band together and encourage and strengthen one another. We need to fight for one another! Today, find somebody in need of encouragement in our army and cheer them on in some way!

Therefore, take up the full armor of God, so that you will be able to resist in the evil day, and having done everything, to stand firm.

— EPHESIANS 6:13

AUGUST 27

"Each a testimony to the Redeemer leading us forth"

Even believers in Christ can be susceptible to the schemes of the enemy. His most devious scheme? To divide the body against itself! Here is a remedy. Let us remember that *he* is the enemy, *not* people. And let us purpose to put on forgiveness—always—toward one another. And let us see one another as Father sees us. If He calls a believer precious, so should we, whether we agree with one another or not!

Let us look upon other believers—even those we dislike or disagree with—as precious testimonies of God's great redeeming love. Let us put on love for one another today.

> Any kingdom divided against itself is laid waste; and any city or house divided against itself will not stand.

> — MATTHEW 12:25

AUGUST 28

"By the blood of the Lamb Satan's work is undone"

How do we overcome the lies of the enemy? By the word of our testimony, by the blood of the Lamb, and by not fearing the laying down of our own lives for our faith. The bottom line is that the blood of Jesus paid our debt and defeated the enemy. Period! When we come to believe this truth and receive it, we see the power of the enemy as being merely the power of deception. He is defeated by truth, and the blood of Jesus—the Way, the Truth, and the Life—secures our victory over those lies.

Let us put down the lies today and walk in the truth of the power of the blood of Christ!

And they overcame him because of the blood of the Lamb and because of the word of their testimony, and they did not love their life even when faced with death.

— REVELATION 12:11

AUGUST 29

"I'm a testimony that the blood has overcome"

Believer, how do you see yourself today? Have you been redeemed? What if you stumble and fall into some sin today? What then? The great news is that *nothing changes*! You are *still* redeemed! The victorious new creation knows this and, rather than wallowing in self-pity and defeat and staying down on the ground, picks themselves back up and dusts off by repenting, then continues to walk as the new creation they still are! The only failure is to fall and simply not get back up. That is not who you are! Keep getting back up and keep heading toward Jesus!

Today, be the testimony to the power of His grace that you truly are!

By faith Abel offered to God a better sacrifice than Cain, through which he obtained the testimony that he was righteous, God testifying about his gifts, and through faith, though he is dead, he still speaks.

— HEBREWS 11:4

AUGUST 30

"We are Your children"

Listen to the song "Blessed Be The Name Of The Lord" from the album *The Worshipper's Collection, Vol. 2.*

We are your children.
You are our righteousness.
We are Your children.
Jesus, we will confess

That You are the Lord!
We will give You glory.
Jesus, You are the Lord!
We will give You praise declaring;
Blessed be the Name of the Lord,
Now and forevermore!
Blessed be the Name of the Lord,
Now and forevermore!
Send down Your Spirit!
Fill us all up with the glory of the Lord!
Send down Your Spirit!
Jesus is the Lord and He reigns forevermore!
Blessed be the Name of the Lord,
Now and forevermore!

Blessed be the Name of the Lord,
Now and forevermore!
Blessed be the Name of the Lord!
Blessed be the Name of the,
Blessed be the Name of the Lord!

We are Your servants.
You are the reigning King.
We are Your servants.
Victoriously we will sing

It is always good for us to remind ourselves of who and whose we are. Born again, we become new creations in Christ. Our old selves are crucified with Christ, buried with Him, and ultimately we rise again as new creations, leaving our old selves in the grave! Victory comes when we begin to think as new creations.

Let us spend time today identifying ourselves according to who Father says we are. One of the best ways to remind ourselves of who Father says we are is to simply commune with Him in praise. Praise Him for who *He* is and discover who you are as His child!

I have been crucified with Christ; and it is no longer I who live, but Christ lives in me; and the life which I now live in the flesh I live by faith in the Son of God, who loved me and gave Himself up for me.

— GALATIANS 2:20

"You are our Righteousness"

We could never earn our way into right standing with God. We all try in various ways, thinking we can make God accept us based on our performance. That is no way to live! We are children of the Most High God who wanted us so badly that He gave His only Son to bridge the gap sin had left between us and Himself! For us to think we must perform to gain His love and acceptance is for us to say there is no power in His redeeming love. Freedom comes by stopping the performance and simply accepting the free gift of salvation and love He offers us. Freedom comes from simply *being* His child!

Simply be his child today.

He made Him who knew no sin to be sin on our behalf, so that we might become the righteousness of God in Him.

— 2 CORINTHIANS 5:21

SEPTEMBER

SEPTEMBER 1

"We are Your children - Jesus, we will confess"

When we make confession with our mouths that go against the lies of the enemy—even when we do not *feel* the truth—we are actively taking dominion over our very being. With our physical strength we rule over our tongue. With our mental capacity we declare the truth to be what God calls true. With our will we rule over our emotions by desiring to feel what Father feels. Honest confession provides a practical way to overcome the lies of the enemy, a way that quiets every means the enemy has of speaking his subtle lies.

I encourage you to praise God today—whether you feel like it or not—and, in the process, take dominion over your own being and put the enemy under your feet.

But what does it say? "The Word is near you, in your mouth and in your heart"—that is, the word of faith which we are preaching, that if you confess with your mouth Jesus as Lord, and believe in your heart that God raised Him from the dead, you will be saved; for with the heart a person believes, resulting in righteousness, and with the mouth he confesses, resulting in salvation.

— ROMANS 10:8-10

SEPTEMBER 2

"Jesus we will confess that You are the Lord"

When the enemy comes with his lies and tries to confuse us and bring division between us and our Father, it is vital that we remember our position in Christ. We belong to Jesus, and He is our Lord. Jesus conquered sin and death for us, so we are victorious regardless of our circumstances. Jesus is Lord. That is enough!

Make that confession today in physical words, in emotional responses, in attitude, and in thought.

For this reason also, God highly exalted Him, and bestowed on Him the name which is above every name, so that at the name of Jesus every knee will bow, of those who are in heaven and on earth and under the earth, and that every tongue will confess that Jesus Christ is Lord, to the glory of God the Father.

— PHILIPPIANS 2:9-11

SEPTEMBER 3

"We will give You glory"

What does it mean to give God glory? Simply put, giving God glory is thanking Him for who He is and for what He has done, and, if we go a step further, thanking Him for all He is *going* to do!

Let us practice giving God glory today by extolling his virtues in our entire being. When appropriate, tell others why you are thankful to God. Speak to your soul and declare to yourself all the reasons you are grateful to God. Spend time worshiping Him in song if you have the chance. Simply give God glory today!

> Ascribe to the Lord the glory due to His name;
>> Worship the Lord in holy array

— PSALM 29:2

SEPTEMBER 4

"You are the Lord and we will give You praise declaring"

Jesus is Lord, pure and simple, but how do we respond if the circumstances of life do not match that truth? We must determine that Jesus is Lord no matter what! Sounds simple, but it's not always so easy, because life has a way of throwing curve balls that leave us reeling and wondering where Jesus is in the chaos. When harsh circumstances occur, we must be quick to put on the truth that God is in control—Jesus is Lord —no matter what. We must see from His perspective and remember that, like the sun still shines even though the storm rages, our God *is* with us through the personal storms of life.

Today, live in that Sonshine by declaring the Lordship of Jesus Christ as you put on the garment of praise today!

> The Spirit of the Lord God is upon me,
>> Because the Lord has anointed me
>> To bring good news to the afflicted;
>> He has sent me to bind up the brokenhearted,
>> To proclaim liberty to captives
>> And freedom to prisoners;
>> To proclaim the favorable year of the Lord
>> And the day of vengeance of our God;
>> To comfort all who mourn,
>> To grant those who mourn in Zion,
>> Giving them a garland instead of ashes,
>> The oil of gladness instead of mourning,
>> The mantle of praise instead of a spirit of fainting.
>> So they will be called oaks of righteousness,
>> The planting of the Lord, that He may be glorified.

> — ISAIAH 61:1-3

SEPTEMBER 5

"Blessed be the name of the Lord now and forevermore"

What do you think of when you hear the word *blessed*? I think of the holiness—the perfection—of God. I also think that the blessed person has been granted some great fortune or favor. Sometimes, the word denotes a feeling of happiness. When I think of God and my need to worship Him, I think of Him in exactly those ways! He is perfect and He is perfecting me. I give Him the highest place of favor in my existence, and He does the same for me! I believe God is ecstatically happy in who He is, and I believe He is ecstatically happy that I am His! Bless the Lord in all your ways today!

Blessed be the name of the Lord
From this time forth and forever.

— PSALM 113:2

SEPTEMBER 6

"Send down Your Spirit"

Where the Spirit of the Lord is there is freedom! What does that tell us? Freedom is *always* available, always *with* us! The Lord has sent His Holy Spirit to fill us with power and to be our constant companion, infusing us with His identity! This is valuable information to the new creation. What is the sign of that filling? You will know a tree by its what? You will know a tree by the fruit it bears. Let us constantly seek to be filled with the Holy Spirit.

Bear the fruit of the Spirit by daily inviting Him to fill you with all He is. And remember, freedom is always within reach because He is always with you!

Now the Lord is the Spirit, and where the Spirit of the Lord is, there is liberty.

— 2 CORINTHIANS 3:17

But the fruit of the Spirit is love, joy, peace, patience, kindness, goodness, faithfulness, gentleness, self-control; against such things there is no law.

— GALATIANS 5:22-23

~

SEPTEMBER 7

"Fill us all up with the glory of the Lord"

The glory of the Lord is the weight of His presence. Sometimes we feel the Lord's presence, and sometimes we do not. Our feelings are actually beside the point, because He *never* leaves us or forsakes us. When we acknowledge the Lord's presence we are acting as the new creations we are. More often than not, when we affirm the Lord's presence by a mental step of faith, our attitude follows suit, and our feelings follow suit, and our behavior follows suit!

By faith, let us acknowledge the Lord's presence in all our ways today and truly walk as the new creations we are. In this manner, we truly become conduits of His glory, and our lives — whether we realize it or not — affect those we come in contact with! Be a vessel of His glory today. Just be who you are called to be!

Trust in the Lord with all your heart

    And do not lean on your own understanding.

    In all your ways acknowledge Him,

    And He will make your paths straight.

— PROVERBS 3:5-6

SEPTEMBER 8

"Send down Your Spirit"

When walking with the Lord, it is vitally important for us to remember that the Holy Spirit is *always* with us — even when we forget or don't *feel* His presence. This is where our faith must kick into gear, so to speak! Just because we do not sense His presence does not mean He is not there. Either He is always present or never present. We cannot have it both ways based only on how we feel in any given moment. God is faithful — and that faithfulness is always with us!

Today, let us meditate on this truth. Let us practice walking in faith during times when we do not sense God's presence.

Now the Lord is the Spirit, and where the Spirit of the Lord is, there is liberty.

— 2 CORINTHIANS 3:17

SEPTEMBER 9

"Jesus is the Lord and He reigns forevermore"

Everything we see with our human eyes will one day pass away. Every single thing from the earth to our bodies are simply wood, hay, and stubble, easily consumed by fire. But there is good news! The greatest truth of all is that true reality is that which is spiritual. God is Spirit. We, in our core identity, are spirit. This means we will endure—even when everything around us is burning away or crumbling!

Let us walk today as those who know the greater reality of who and whose we are, and that *nothing* changes whether we live or whether we die! Let us build our lives on the Firm Foundation!

> According to the grace of God which was given to me, like a wise master builder I laid a foundation, and another is building on it. But each man must be careful how he builds on it. For no man can lay a foundation other than the one which is laid, which is Jesus Christ.
>
> — 1 CORINTHIANS 3:10-11

SEPTEMBER 10

"Blessed be the name of the Lord now and forevermore"

Let today be a day of intentional praise to the Lord. Ask the Holy Spirit to remind you of all the blessings He has bestowed upon your life. Let this attitude of gratitude permeate all you say, think, and do today. Thank Him for your very existence. Praise Him for your salvation and deliverance. Exalt Him in word and thought and song and expression. Focus on the name of the Lord and what His name means to you. Give God glory and bless His name today!

> He said, "Naked I came from my mother's womb,
>   And naked I shall return there.
>   The Lord gave and the Lord has taken away.
>   Blessed be the name of the Lord."
>
> — JOB 1:21

SEPTEMBER 11

"We are Your servants"

Jesus came to serve mankind by laying down His life. But He also washed the feet of others—the lowliest of tasks usually reserved for the lowest servant or slave. Jesus served by giving of His time and energy to express value to others. Jesus served His Father by seeking to save the lost and dying.

Let this be our attitude today—to serve as Jesus did. In so doing, the sermon we preach to those around us will express more than our feeble words ever could.

But it is not this way among you, but whoever wishes to

become great among you shall be your servant; and whoever wishes to be first among you shall be slave of all.

— MARK 10:43-44

SEPTEMBER 12

"You are the reigning King"

The world in which we live has a way of distracting us from the truth—the enemy sees to that! Unjust rulers impose their will upon entire nations and it seems there is nothing we can do about it. We have all seen criminals go free in the name of justice. Fortune and riches fall upon some of the most perverse people, while we suffer for the sake of righteousness. Life is not fair. That is simple reality. But, our God is in control. That is the hope we must cling to. He will use whatever He will to bring beauty from the ashes of our lives, even our suffering. This I know: our God wastes nothing and He is *good*, regardless of what the enemy might try to dissuade us from that truth.

Let us put off the lies today and put on the truth. Our God reigns regardless of the fairness of life!

But I say to you, love your enemies and pray for those who persecute you, so that you may be sons of your Father who is in heaven; for He causes His sun to rise on the evil and the good, and sends rain on the righteous and the unrighteous.

— MATTHEW 5:44-45

SEPTEMBER 13

"We are Your servants"

Today, let us put our money where our mouth is. We call ourselves servants of the Most High God, and we say we want to be like Jesus—who was the greatest Servant of all—so let's be very intentional as we go about our day. Let us look for—be keenly sensitive to—ways we can serve others without even saying a word. Be ready to give a helping hand, or open a door, or carry a load, or give a warm smile. Service looks like Jesus. Let's be about *His* business today, in attitude as well as action!

Serve the Lord with gladness;
Come before Him with joyful singing.

— PSALM 100: 2

SEPTEMBER 14

"Victoriously we will sing"

There is something about singing that lifts the heart. It's a lot like laughter—a good medicine for the soul. Even those of us with less-than-stellar voices still love to sing. Ever catch yourself abandoning your soul to a song with gusto in the shower? We all have! In singing to the Lord, you take captive every thought. You also bathe your physical strength and emotions in good and profitable activity—giving the lies of the enemy no place to land!

Find time today to sing your praise and thanksgiving to the Lord. Use your drive time to sing. Use the shower! Steal away for even a couple of minutes during break time. Just sing!

I will give thanks to the Lord according to His righteousness
And will sing praise to the name of the Lord Most High.

— PSALM 7:17

SEPTEMBER 15

"When I took up the cross of Christ I knew I would suffer"

Listen to the song "Take Me There" from the album *The Worshipper's Collection Vol. 2.*

When I took up the cross of Christ,
I knew I would suffer.
When He took me from death to life,
He gave me love like no other.
Lord, all I know is that I love just being with You.
I will follow You, Lord, it doesn't matter where.

All I know is that I love and want to lift You higher, Lord.
Won't You take me there?
There, where the Lamb will lay down with the lion,
There, where there is no pain or strife,
There, where there is no night, no dying,
There, where Living Water flows and the Lamb alone is Light.

There, where the Lord, Jesus Christ will reign forever,
There, where we will worship around His throne,
There, where the blood bought Church will come together,
There, where all the redeemed of the Lord will rejoice before Him
ever,
There, where the Father says, "Well done! Welcome into your
forever home"

To live is Christ, to die is gain,
Life is found in dying.
The driest times make for sweeter rain,
Simple love satisfying.
Lord, all I know is that I love just being with You.
Rain or shine or confusion in the air,

When we become Christ followers, we become bearers of
the cross. By the bearing of the cross of Christ in our lives, we
identify with Him and, in a sense, bear Christ to the world
around us. That means we carry Christ with us wherever we
go, to whomever we are with. We bear Christ to others
through our attitudes and actions and words—through our
kindness. And the greatest expression of Christ through our
lives? Bearing His love to those we come in contact with.

How can you bear Christ to others today. Be sensitive to
the Holy Spirit and *bear* in mind that you are a Christ *bearer!*

Then Jesus said to His disciples, "If anyone wishes to come
after Me, he must deny himself, and take up his cross and
follow Me."

— MATTHEW 16:24

SEPTEMBER 16

"When He took me from death to life, He gave me love like no other"

Love that is not expressed is not love. I can tell my wife or children with my words how much I love them, but if those words are not backed up by my actions, I am no more than a clanging cymbal—an annoying noisemaker! The Kingdom of God is more than words, it is love expressed, ultimately, by the laying down of life.

Let us focus today on the depth of the reality of true love, and let us ponder how we can best lay down our lives for others today. For God so loved the world that He *gave.*

> For God so loved the world, that He gave His only begotten Son, that whoever believes in Him shall not perish, but have eternal life.

> — JOHN 3:16

SEPTEMBER 17

"Lord, all I know is that I love just being with You"

I have certain friends who I enjoy being with simply because they make me happy and glad to be alive. With these friends, part of the joy I feel comes from the knowledge that I can completely relax and be myself in their presence. They see all my

frailties and continue to welcome my fellowship—relationship—
no matter what. Knowing Father is like that, completely.
Knowing I am loved and accepted by my Father helps me release
my burdens and frees me from the shackles of sin. Knowing I am
loved and accepted by God makes me want to just be with Him.

Take time to just *be* with Father today, and enjoy His presence *all day long.*

> You will make known to me the path of life;
> In Your presence is fullness of joy;
> In Your right hand there are pleasures forever.

— PSALM 16:11

SEPTEMBER 18

"I will follow You, Lord, it doesn't matter where"

A few years ago, I was invited to speak before a state legis-
lature concerning same sex marriage. I asked several friends to
go with me, and none would. I felt fearful having to face what I
knew I would for taking a stand. It broke my heart that none
would go with me. My oldest son volunteered to go, and he
was only 15 or 16 at the time. An amazing thing took place in
my heart and mind. Completely overwhelmed with pride in my
son's courage, I was amazed at the calm assurance this brought
my soul. The fear was suddenly gone, because I realized I
would not be alone. It is knowing Father is with us—complete
love—that banishes fear from our minds. The Lord used my
son to remind me that, regardless of whether I am physically

alone or not, I will never be alone through any circumstance of life.

Today, let us focus on the Lord's nearness to us, and watch fear subside in the process.

There is no fear in love; but perfect love casts out fear, because fear involves punishment, and the one who fears is not perfected in love.

— 1 JOHN 4:18

~

SEPTEMBER 19

"All I know is that I love and want to lift You higher, Lord, won't You take me there?"

When I worship God my entire being becomes focused on Father like a laser. In that focus, the enemy has no place to land a dart of accusation or any semblance of a lie. It is when I lift up the name of the Lord in worship that I soar over the cares of life and see it from the King's point of view. In that sense, life is all about the Kingdom of God. The Kingdom of God encompasses all God is and, at the same time, is limitless!

Let us lift up the Lord in thought, attitude, and active worship throughout the day. In the process, we will soar to heights unattainable any other way.

Yet those who wait for the Lord
    Will gain new strength;

They will mount up with wings like eagles,
They will run and not get tired,
They will walk and not become weary.

— ISAIAH 40:31

SEPTEMBER 20

"There, where the Lamb will lay down with the lion"

When the world around us seems to be in chaos, how do we find peace? Knowing we are citizens of the Kingdom of God reminds us that we walk in a realm that transcends human senses. Regardless of the political winds of the day, regardless of the emotional whims of those around us, and regardless of our personal circumstances, our God reigns! If that is true, then grace abounds to us every instant of every day. The only thing keeping us from God's grace is our own choice not to receive it.

Believe and receive today.

Let the peace of Christ rule in your hearts, to which indeed you were called in one body; and be thankful.

— COLOSSIANS 3:15

~

SEPTEMBER 21

"There, where there is no pain or strife"

Can you imagine a world without pain or strife? It really is something to look forward to in eternity, isn't it? But reality is that, due to sin, there will always be pain and strife in this world. That is why we need to have a Kingdom perspective, one that says, "Whatever Satan means for evil, God will use for good." When pain comes, a kingdom perspective says, "Now I have an opportunity to experience God's grace, and comfort, and healing." When strife comes, we have the opportunity to experience reconciliation and deeper relationship and, always, a deeper outpouring of God's grace. Let us not view life from the stance of our humanity or that of the enemy. May we give those perspectives mere glances. But let us give the grace of God our unbridled gaze.

See life from the King's perspective today.

> Consider it all joy, my brethren, when you encounter various trials, knowing that the testing of your faith produces endurance.
>
> — JAMES 1:2-3

SEPTEMBER 22

"There, where there is no night, no dying"

Life has a way of knocking us down sometimes. Disappointments come. Betrayal is a reality. Disillusionment occurs. Death calls. Life is full of sorrows and tears, sometimes to the point that we want to lay down and give up. As new creations —Kingdom citizens—we must walk in the big-picture King-dom-reality. God will use our disappointments to encourage us. He will use the times of betrayal to help us trust. He will use times of disillusionment to bring us deeper into the Light. He will use even death to show us abundant life.

Wherever you find yourself today, walk in the reality of the big picture and see victory invade even the most dire of circumstances.

> But if we walk in the Light as He Himself is in the Light, we have fellowship with one another, and the blood of Jesus His Son cleanses us from all sin.
>
> — 1 JOHN 1:7

SEPTEMBER 23

"There, where Living Water flows and the Lamb alone is Light"

At times in my life, I have become so overwhelmed with busyness that I lose sight of the obvious—God is in control whether I see it or not! It is during such times that He reminds me to simplify my life in every way. How do I do that? By getting to the lowest common denominator of the Kingdom —*love*. In any given situation, I can ask a simple series of questions and find peace and wisdom in the process. How can I love God in this situation? How can I love the other party in this situation? How can I love myself, define myself, as Father does? When I answer those questions, my attitude changes and I see from the King's perspective, and life is abundant in that place!

Today, try getting back to the lowest common denominator of love.

And he answered, "You shall love the Lord your God with all your heart, and with all your soul, and with all your strength, and with all your mind; and your neighbor as yourself."

— LUKE 10:27

SEPTEMBER 24

"There, where the Lord, Jesus Christ will reign forever"

Is there any place or circumstance that Jesus does not reign? If we listen to the lies of the enemy, the answer would be *yes*, but if we walk in the truth of the Light of Jesus Christ, we know that Jesus reigns *no matter what*! How do we incorporate that truth in our lives when, in today's culture, the enemy seems to bombard us from every angle? God sets all of existence in motion and His hand governs everything. As new creations—Citizens of the Kingdom—we must walk in our true identity in order to see the rule and reign of Christ. Victory comes when we are able to see past the smoke and mirrors of the enemy's lies and grasp that the Lord uses even the enemy's feeble deceptions for our good, if we allow Him to.

I urge you, walk as a citizen of the Kingdom of God today. See life from His point of view!

The Lord reigns, He is clothed with majesty;
The Lord has clothed and girded Himself with strength;
Indeed, the world is firmly established, it will not be moved.

— PSALM 93:1

SEPTEMBER 25

"There, where we will worship around His throne"

We often talk about one day worshiping around the throne of God, and we will, but let us practice the atmosphere of heaven in all we say, think, and do this day. If reverence and awe surround the throne of God, then let reverence and awe for His earthly presence in our lives permeate all we say, think, and do. Our attitude of awe will flavor everything we engage in during the course of this day. How awesome it is for God's presence to so enrich and inhabit our attitudes that it affects everyone we come in contact with—whether they know it or not, whether *we* know it or not!

Let us join with the atmosphere of heaven today by altering our attitudes in reverence and awe of God.

And all the angels were standing around the throne and around the elders and the four living creatures; and they fell on their faces before the throne and worshiped God, saying, "Amen, blessing and glory and wisdom and thanksgiving and honor and power and might, be to our God forever and ever. Amen."

— REVELATION 7:11-12

SEPTEMBER 26

"There, where the blood bought Church will come together"

In America, I look around the body of Christ—from various denominations and camps of doctrine—and see so many different displays of God's hand. Wouldn't it be something if every one of us suddenly realized we are on the same team? Wouldn't it be absolutely awesome if we, all at once, realized the body of Christ is more than what the American church has made it to be? Wouldn't it be something if the body of Christ simultaneously realized that the Kingdom of God is much bigger than we imagined and we are all Citizens of that Kingdom? We have all been bought with the same price—the blood of Christ. Let us begin thinking like we believe that and watch the body of Christ take on a whole new meaning to us as the church. It has to begin somewhere. It might as well be in you and me!

Today, consider how you might bridge the gap between yourself and your fellow Citizens of the Kingdom. Then, take a step in that direction.

For just as we have many members in one body and all the members do not have the same function, so we, who are many, are one body in Christ, and individually members one of another.

— ROMANS 12:4-5

SEPTEMBER 27

*"There, where all the redeemed of the Lord will rejoice before
Him ever"*

When we understand who we are because of whose we are, life ceases to be boring! At least, that is my perspective. Rather than constantly battling discouragement and temptation, I now see life from a whole new point of view. Even the enemy's discouragement causes me to think, "What are you about to do next, Father, that would make the enemy resort to that idiotic little lie?" or "What truth do you want to reveal that the enemy is trying to hide with this inane temptation?" We are redeemed. If that is true, all the old things have passed away and the slate is clean!

Today, let's purpose to walk in God's reality in spite of our circumstances and in spite of the conventional wisdom of this world! We have every reason to rejoice in *this* life!

Let the redeemed of the Lord say so,
Whom He has redeemed from the hand of the adversary.

— PSALM 107:2

"There, where the Father says, 'Well done!'"

Our Father is good, no matter what. How do I know this? Personal experience! When my children were young, it seemed I was always comforting them from the trauma of a fall that resulted in a scrape and bruised ego. More often than not, that comfort was accompanied by me wiping away the dirt they had accumulated and binding up their wounds. Never once did I send them from my fatherly presence to cleanse themselves or bind their own wounds. I, their father, did that for them — and I am an earthly Father! Our heavenly Father is so much better than that, yet we sell Him short by seeing Him through the filter of our earthly fathers. Stop that, now! See Father as He is — always inviting us to bare our wounds and failures to Him, always ready to cleanse us and bind our wounds.

Today, let our faith rise to meet our needs, and let us walk as children who *know* their Father is good!

> If you then, being evil, know how to give good gifts to your children, how much more will your Father who is in heaven give what is good to those who ask Him!
>
> — MATTHEW 7:11

SEPTEMBER 29

"Welcome into your forever home"

When does eternity with Jesus begin, when we die or in the here and now? Of course the answer is that we are already living in eternity. Yes, we have a wonderful existence to look forward to in heaven, but we do not have to wait until eternity to begin. We do not have to wait until we die to enjoy the presence of God or sit at the feast of the King. We can do that now, today!

Let us practice the presence of God today by simply believing He is with us through every step, good or bad. And rejoice!

> But just as it is written, "Things which eye has not seen and ear has not heard, and which have not entered the heart of man, all that God has prepared for those who love him."
>
> — 1 CORINTHIANS 2:9

SEPTEMBER 30

"To live is Christ, to die is gain"

We all face death. That is the way it is. We can choose to either see life from our weak and feeble human perspective or from the King's perspective. There is life even in death. Jesus died to give us life. We died to our old sinful existence and were born again into eternal life. We see death in some of our dreams and visions, but even then, our God is able to show us His point of view and bring life in the midst of those deaths. Abundant life really is a matter of perspective. One perspective leads to despair while the other leads to grace.

Which will you choose to see life from today?

Truly, truly, I say to you, unless a grain of wheat falls into the earth and dies, it remains alone; but if it dies, it bears much fruit.

— JOHN 12:24

OCTOBER

OCTOBER 1

"Life is found in dying"

Life is full of wonderful paradoxes. There is no joy without sorrow. There is no healing without wounds. There would be no peace without chaos. There would be no hope unless we knew despair. Those statements sound so contrary to one another yet this idea is one of the wonders of the Kingdom of God. He is able to take our deepest griefs and make them points of great joy. He is able to take our greatest failures and bring great victory from them.

Today, let us determine anew to live in the realm of the King in spite of our circumstances. Let us enjoy the wonder of His great mystery and amazing ways.

There are three things which are too wonderful for me,

Four which I do not understand:
The way of an eagle in the sky,
The way of a serpent on a rock,
The way of a ship in the middle of the sea,
And the way of a man with a maid.

— PROVERBS 30:18-19

OCTOBER 2

"The driest times make for sweeter rain"

This past year, our region suffered a severe summer with no rain and more than twenty consecutive days of over one hundred degree weather. We were weary of the heat and concerned about the numerous consequences of getting no rain. Our water sources were running low. Parasites were growing in the stagnant lakes, causing health risks. Ponds were running dry and causing ranchers to sell off entire herds of cattle. And fire wrought havoc in our area due to the dried grass and brush. Things are different now. We just experienced four days of constant rain. The ponds are full. The rivers and lakes are full. Everything is wonderfully green. And everyone's hearts are visibly lifted. We should never look down upon the dry times of life, because they make the rain all the sweeter.

Apply this attitude to your emotional and spiritual life, and enjoy the rain!

So rejoice, O sons of Zion,
And be glad in the Lord your God;
For He has given you the early rain for your vindication.

And He has poured down for you the rain,
The early and latter rain as before.

— JOEL 2:23

OCTOBER 3

"Simple love satisfying"

Isn't it amazing how we long for valuable material items but tend to find greater joy in the simplest places? How many times did I give my small children lavish gifts only to find them playing with the boxes they came in? Love is not quantified by things. In the Kingdom of God, we could lose all earthly possessions and still be joyfully happy, because we know that, in spite of our circumstances, nothing changes in our relationship with God.

Today, let us enjoy Him and be like children who enjoy His presence more than the trappings of the material life.

For what does it profit a man to gain the whole world, and forfeit his soul?

— MARK 8:36

OCTOBER 4

"Lord, all I know is that I love just being with You"

When I am with my children—especially now that they are

adults and I no longer get to see them on a regular basis—I relish every minute of our time together. My desire is to not waste time on trivial matters but to simply focus on *being* with them. My joy is in their presence, and that joy is enhanced when we walk in sweet relationship with one another, sharing our life together. I feel that way and I am an *earthly father!* How much more capacity does our heavenly Father have to enjoy our presence and relate to us?

Today, embrace this reality and spend time simply *being* with Father.

> Grace to you and peace from God our Father and the Lord Jesus Christ.
>
> — 1 CORINTHIANS 1:3

OCTOBER 5

"Rain or shine or confusion in the air"

The enemy loves to get us so focused on our surroundings that we miss the joy of the journey. Rather than gripe about the rain, thank God for its sustenance and the cleansing it brings. Rather than complain about excessive winds, thank God for the way He uses the wind to scatter seeds and power turbines and cleanse the air. Rather than murmur against God for allowing the harsh circumstances of your life, thank Him for yet another opportunity to receive His grace and experience true intimacy.

Walk in the Kingdom perspective today!

Therefore humble yourselves under the mighty hand of God, that He may exalt you at the proper time, casting all your anxiety on Him, because He cares for you.

— 1 PETER 5:6-7

OCTOBER 6

"Like a star in the heavens"

When we look into the sky on a moonless night, the stars seem far too countless to fathom their number, yet no two stars are exactly alike! When God made you, He made you that uniquely. There is no one like you in the entire existence of the universe! How special! How precious you are that He would make such a concerted effort to guarantee your special place in this world, in this universe, in His heart! Do you understand the depth of what this means to you on a personal level? Can you fathom the depth of value and worth this bestows upon you? Does this knowledge cause you to want to rise up and bless Him? Does it cause you to rise up and ask for more and more clarity concerning your true identity and purpose in life?

Today, be like the star in the heavens and shine brightly out of the sheer joy of knowing who and whose you are.

Lift up your eyes on high
    And see who has created these stars,
    The One who leads forth their host by number,
    He calls them all by name;
    Because of the greatness of His might and the strength of
His power,

Not one of them is missing.

OCTOBER 7

"Like a flower in the spring"

Have you ever come across a field of nothing but flowers? In the Oklahoma springtime, we have large areas of brilliant red Indian Paintbrushes that adorn our fields. In Texas, they have the famous Bluebonnets gracing acre after acre with their glorious blue brilliance. Yet when you look closely at each individual flower, they are as varied as they are numerous! How amazing is that? As new creations, we are like those flowers. God has placed us in the body of Christ where we appear to be one of many, yet as we look closer at each individual, we see the massive creativity of our God—each of us is seen by God as completely unique and special! That makes me feel very loved and very much a part of the greater whole we call the body of Christ.

He took the time to make you just for Himself. Glory in that today! Walk in the spiritual confidence of one who knows who they are and who has no doubt about whose they are!

And who of you by being worried can add a single hour to his life? And why are you worried about clothing? Observe how the lilies of the field grow; they do not toil nor do they spin.

— MATTHEW 6:27-28

OCTOBER 8

"Like a bluebird in the forest with a joyous song to sing"

One morning this past spring, my wife was sitting on our front porch just taking in nature. As she sat there, a bird begin to sing, and then another and another and another, until there was an absolute symphony taking place in the air surrounding our home. It was as if all of creation had spontaneously erupted in a song of magnificent praise to our God. Her heart was deeply blessed as she pondered how the Lord had done this just for her.

Take time today to watch for and listen for the little bless-ings—the little hints—of God's deep love and care for you. Don't take lightly the small, seemingly insignificant nuances of His presence and grace. Let Him speak and show off His love for you in any way He chooses!

> But let all who take refuge in You be glad,
>> Let them ever sing for joy;
>> And may You shelter them,
>> That those who love Your name may exult in You.

> — PSALM 5:11

OCTOBER 9

"Like valleys in the mountains"

We all love the experience of looking down upon creation

from a lofty mountaintop, but once there, we realize how barren the peak truly is. It is when we look down at the beauty of the valley that we see the lush green flora that nurtures the world with life. Mountaintops are great vistas from which to see, but life is truly lived in the valleys. Real life is down where people are. Real life is not on the mountaintops—it must be embraced in the valleys to be truly enjoyed, truly lived.

Do not despise the valleys you walk through today. Rather, try to see from the King's vantage point (like a little view from the top) yet live your life fully right where you are. This is the place of victory, and *that*, my friends, is where he has prepared the feast He invites us to enjoy *in this life!*

> Let every valley be lifted up,
>> And every mountain and hill be made low;
>> And let the rough ground become a plain,
>> And the rugged terrain a broad valley;
>> Then the glory of the Lord will be revealed,
>> And all flesh will see it together;
>> For the mouth of the Lord has spoken.

— ISAIAH 40:4-5

OCTOBER 10

"Like waves upon the sea"

The waves of the sea are as varied as anything on earth. No two waves are the same. No two waves have the same power. Some waves bring joy—as when ridden by a surfer. Some waves bring devastation—as with a sudden tsunami in a populated area. Some waves are small. Some waves are huge. Some waves break slowly with a gentle flourish while others pound the shore with relentless force and fury. Sometimes, the circumstances of life can be like the waves of the sea. The waves of circumstances are best endured from the vantage point of the King. When we can see what He sees, the wave that threatens destruction can actually bring cleansing, life, and unexpected opportunities to experience God's grace.

Look beyond life's devastation and see the hope of His presence.

> Deep calls to deep at the sound of Your waterfalls;
> All Your breakers and Your waves have rolled over me.

> — PSALM 42:7

OCTOBER 11

"They belong together in a perfect way just like my Lord and me"

When we think of words which are connected with some other word, it is difficult to separate the two. When I think of *soup* I also instantly think of *sandwich*, because they go together in my mind. When I think of *love* I immediately think of *marriage*, because they go together in my mind (due to the old Frank Sinatra standard "Love and Marriage"). When I think of the Lord I experience the same phenomenon. When I think of Him, I think of me and how we were meant for one another, how we go together like soup and sandwich or love and marriage! The word *inseparable* also comes to mind. Sounds silly and a bit simplistic, perhaps, but it is true.

Ponder this today as you allow the Holy Spirit to soak this concept in your heart and mind.

> For I am convinced that neither death, nor life, nor angels, nor principalities, nor things present, nor things to come, nor powers, nor height, nor depth, nor any other created thing, will be able to separate us from the love of God, which is in Christ Jesus our Lord.

> — ROMANS 8:38-39

∿

OCTOBER 12

"Hand in hand dear, Jesus, all along the way"

We probably all remember times from childhood when a parent took us by the hand and gave us a sense of security and joy like nothing else. If you have ever taken a child by the hand, you know the joy it brings you as a parent or caregiver. Our relationship with Jesus is like that yet so much more. When we place our hand in His, we become like trusting children. We gain a sense of security and joy knowing we are cared for. At the same time, we must understand the sheer joy He takes in *us* in such moments. If we feel those things toward our own children, how much more does He feel them toward us?

Ponder this thought today and practice walking hand in hand with Jesus.

Then some children were brought to Him so that He might lay His hands on them and pray; and the disciples rebuked them. But Jesus said, "Let the children alone, and do not hinder them from coming to Me; for the kingdom of heaven belongs to such as these."

— MATTHEW 19:13-14

~

OCTOBER 13

"Hand in hand, dear Jesus, each and every day"

Not one day goes by without the Lord's presence in our lives. Not even one moment goes by without His presence surrounding us. The problem comes when we refuse to acknowledge His presence, or we simply become so consumed with our lives that we forget He's there. It's one this to forget He's always with us and quite another to choose to ignore that truth. This is where faith comes into play. We simply step out in faith and trust Him to be there, in spite of our feelings or circumstances. In this place of trust, we can live and see the entirety of our existence through the filter of His presence in and with us.

Walk with Him today. Talk with Him today. Think of Him today. Just *be* with Him today. Enjoy the fullness of His presence.

You will make known to me the path of life;

In Your presence is fullness of joy;

In Your right hand there are pleasures forever.

— PSALM 16:11

OCTOBER 14

"Hand in hand, dear Jesus"

When I think of someone's hands, I think of many things — care, strength, guidance, work, sacrifice. Relationship is expressed through holding hands. Commitment is expressed through shaking hands with another. And just think of the nail scars in the hands of Jesus. What do his hands communicate?

Today, meditate on the hands of Jesus as a means of discovering more of who He has called *you* to be. Take that personally. Practice being His hands to others today.

> And they came to Bethsaida. And they brought a blind man to Jesus and implored Him to touch him. Taking the blind man by the hand, He brought him out of the village; and after spitting on his eyes and laying His hands on him, He asked him, "Do you see anything?" And he looked up and said, "I see men, for I see them like trees, walking around." Then again He laid His hands on his eyes; and he looked intently and was restored, and began to see everything clearly.

— MARK 8:22-25

OCTOBER 15

*"I love to hear You say, 'Child, I want to wipe away your every
tear'"*

Far too often, we view Father as a cosmic policeman who is
looking for mistakes so He can swoop down with correction
and punishment. I am a dad and that has never been my mode
of operation with my children! I cannot think of a quicker way
to alienate them from me! Our Father wants nothing but what
is best for us! Of course He brings correction. Of course He
brings punishment when necessary. A good father does those
things, but always out of wanting what's best for his child. Our
Father is good. He is the *best* Father. And all He does is born
out of His love for us.

Today, trust His love and respond to others out of it.

He who withholds his rod hates his son,
But he who loves him disciplines him diligently.

— PROVERBS 13:24

OCTOBER 16

"Child, I want take away your every fear"

A wise father helps his children face their fears and see
them for what they are. When one of my sons was a small boy,
he had a very intense fear of storms. He saw weather reports
that showed devastation and destruction and assumed such

259

things came with each and every storm. One spring during an intense thunderstorm, I took my son on a field trip in my truck. I asked him to trust me because I was going to show him a different way to view storms. First, I asked him to look at the raw beauty of the random patterns of lightning. I encouraged him to see the raw power of God displayed in nature. We talked about the purpose of wind and rain and thunder and lightning. We talked about how to see life from a different point of view. Abundant life is found in places like this, where we can see what Father sees regardless of our circumstances.

Get to His vantage point today.

> Therefore everyone who hears these words of Mine and acts on them, may be compared to a wise man who built his house on the rock. And the rain fell, and the floods came, and the winds blew and slammed against that house; and yet it did not fall, for it had been founded on the rock.
>
> — MATTHEW 7:24-25

OCTOBER 17

"Child, I love you so, I want to hold you near"

When my children were smaller it was quite easy to see and identify their emotions. At times, out of pride or fear of rejection, one would refuse to allow me to hold them. Because of my vantage point as Dad, I could help them unravel their tangled thoughts until they were to a place where they would allow me to embrace them, and they, in turn, would embrace me. In that place of intimacy, fear and pride are but a vapor—they have no way to exist when trust is established and connection is made.

Let us tear down any distractions from intimacy with Father today. Let us be wary of fear and pride, and let us vanquish them by being embraced by Father and embracing Him fully!

In this is love, not that we loved God, but that He loved us and sent His Son to be the propitiation for our sins.

— 1 JOHN 4:10

OCTOBER 18

"We belong together - Jesus, my Lord and me"

Think about all Christ did to get to you. He left the riches and glory of heaven. He became a man and was tempted just like you. He suffered the punishment you deserved because of your sin. He paid the debt you could not pay. He redeemed you because He *wanted* you as His own! It sounds like you and Jesus *belong together!* Your salvation—your identity as a new creation—was His dream all along. And now it is your *reality!*

Embrace this depth of belonging today. Own it! Walk in it! Extend it to others!

In Him, you also, after listening to the message of truth, the gospel of your salvation—having also believed, you were sealed in Him with the Holy Spirit of promise, who is given as a pledge of our inheritance, with a view to the redemption of God's own possession, to the praise of His glory.

— EPHESIANS 1:13-14

OCTOBER 19

"Like a sunrise in the morning"

How does it feel to wake up after a night of stormy weather and be presented with a clear sky and bright, shining sun? Refreshing. Healing. Cleansing. Joyful. Walking intimately with Jesus is like that. We may go through a night of storms in our mental, emotional, or spiritual life, but the Son is always there shining! As with a physical thunderstorm, that sunshine is always most apparent after the clouds have cleared, but the sun—the Son—is always there!

Live with this thought at the forefront of your reality today.

I am the Lord, and there is no other;
    Besides Me there is no God.
    I will gird you, though you have not known Me;
    That men may know from the rising to the setting of
the sun
    That there is no one besides Me.
    I am the Lord, and there is no other,
    The One forming light and creating darkness,
    Causing well-being and creating calamity;
    I am the Lord who does all these.

— ISAIAH 45:5-7

OCTOBER 20

"Like a sunset ends the day"

I love to come to the end of a day—productive or otherwise—and see the setting sun. It is a wonderful period that says, "Now you can rest." Knowing Jesus Christ is perpetually like that. Because I am never alone, I always have One to talk to. I always have one to ask the hard questions of. I always have one to go through trials with me. I am literally *never* alone! That gives me peace. That gives me assurance. And one of the most important ways I facilitate that reality? By worshiping God.

Worship Him today and walk in intimate reality with Jesus.

All who dwell on the earth will worship him, everyone whose name has not been written from the foundation of the world in the book of life of the Lamb who has been slain.

— REVELATION 13:8

OCTOBER 21

"Like a mother and a baby"

There is nothing more wonderful and intimate and loving than the way a mother cares for a baby. Having spent the first nine months of life *inside* the mother, the baby has an unbreakable tie and indelible imprint of its mother forever seared in its being. It is the same when we are in Christ as new creations!

We have been given a new nature in Him, and we are indelibly imprinted with His character and nature. By walking in intimate relationship with Him we come to discover and release our true identity in Christ! How awesome is that?

Walk with Him today as one who knows who and whose they are!

> Surely I have composed and quieted my soul;
>> Like a weaned child rests against his mother,
>> My soul is like a weaned child within me.

— PSALM 131:2

OCTOBER 22

"Like a potter and the clay"

Trusting God is not always easy—especially if we have been deeply wounded by one we trust. When we believe that God wants nothing but what is best for us, we trust Him with more and more of our heart and mind and allow Him to use even past wounds to bring deeper intimacy with Him. Our God wastes nothing, but like a master potter, He takes our wounded hearts and molds them to bring healing to the wounds and comfort from the pain. He molds us into who we truly are as new creations in Him.

Today, be His clay and submit to His gentle hands. He will mold something beautiful out of everything you give Him. You must only trust Him.

But now, O Lord, You are our Father,

We are the clay, and You our potter;
And all of us are the work of Your hand.

— ISAIAH 64:8

OCTOBER 23

"Like lightning and the thunder"

Some things just go together—springtime and daffodils, mountains and valleys, thunder and lightning. When we become new creations the things that go together are Jesus and us! We are inseparable whether we recognize it right away or not! Like thunder always follows a crack of lightning, Jesus is always with His new creation. When we are tempted, He is there with a way of escape. When we are wounded, He is there with healing and comfort. When we are blindsided by life and left reeling with questions, He is right there with a gentle, kind hand that leads us through the mess life can be.

Today, trust Him to meet you right where you are, and enjoy His presence through whatever comes your way. You are not alone.

Out from the throne come flashes of lightning and sounds and peals of thunder.

— REVELATION 4:5A

OCTOBER 24

"Like a river and the sea"

The Sea of Galilee feeds northern Israel. Its life-giving water flows down the Jordan River all the way to the Dead Sea. The same water that gives life to the banks of the Jordan and Galilee gives none to the Dead Sea. Why? Because the Dead Sea keeps it all inside! True life requires both giving and receiving — constantly! Our lives in Christ must be like that. I empty myself by making honest confession to Him, and He pours life into me. That cycles leads me to an abundance of life on earth!

Today, let us realize the power of our relationship with Christ and take full advantage of it! Give and receive, and flourish in the process!

How blessed is the man who does not walk in the counsel of
the wicked,
　　Nor stand in the path of sinners,
　　Nor sit in the seat of scoffers!
　　But his delight is in the law of the Lord,
　　And in His law he meditates day and night.
　　He will be like a tree firmly planted by streams of water,
　　Which yields its fruit in its season
　　And its leaf does not wither;
　　And in whatever he does, he prospers.

— PSALM 1:1-3

OCTOBER 25

"They belong together in a perfect way just like my Lord and me"

When we come to understand our position in Christ, we realize we are truly overcomers! Apart from Christ we are victims, but *in* Christ we are victors! When we believe we are who *He* says we are, and receive that truth into our existence, we gain power and authority over the lies of the enemy. As victorious ones, we know that just because we trip and fall does not mean the race is over. On the contrary, the victorious heart gets back up and heads for the finish line—toward Jesus!

Keep your eyes on Him today. Salk in the victory He assured for you on the cross, in the grave, and in the power of His resurrection!

Therefore, since we have so great a cloud of witnesses surrounding us, let us also lay aside every encumbrance and the sin which so easily entangles us, and let us run with endurance the race that is set before us, fixing our eyes on Jesus, the author and perfecter of faith, who for the joy set before Him endured the cross, despising the shame, and has sat down at the right hand of the throne of God.

— HEBREWS 12:1-2

OCTOBER 26

"Here is my heart, Lord - a harvest of grain"

Listen to the song "I Throw My Heart To The Wind" from the album *The Worshipper's Collection Vol. 2.*

Here is my heart Lord, a harvest of grain.
You were the Planter, and You brought the Rain.
Lord of the Harvest, it's time once again to cast all the grain of
my heart to the Wind.

I throw my heart to the Wind to blow out the chaff of my sin.
I throw my heart to the Wind!
Blow through me again and again!
I throw my heart to the Wind to blow out the chaff of my sin.
I throw my heart to the Wind!
Blow through me again and again!

Father has planted a pure holy seed.
But by my own doing, I've sown there a weed.
Sin, like a weed, sprouts again and again.
Can only be killed by a pure holy Wind.

When we walk with Jesus, He plants all kinds of seeds in us—the seed of faith, the seed of identity, the seed of hope, the seed of destiny. As we grow in honest intimacy with Him, He causes those seeds to be watered by the Spirit. As we receive the water of the Spirit, He uses our life experiences to fertilize the soil of our hearts and bring nutrients to feed our souls. Walking in honest and open relationship with Father always brings a harvest in our souls—again and again and again! Who wouldn't desire a harvest of faith and hope and destiny and identity and whatever else Father grows in us?

Enjoy the process today! Receive the planting of the Lord. Receive the watering of the Spirit. Receive the nutrients of life experience and allow it to produce grace in you!

> I am the vine, you are the branches; he who abides in Me and I in him, he bears much fruit, for apart from Me you can do nothing.
>
> — JOHN 15:5

OCTOBER 27

"You were the planter"

When we understand that who we are was imagined, created, and sustained by only one—our Creator—then everything we think about ourselves is seen in a new light. If we have an issue with our identity or reason for existence, shouldn't we be consulting our Maker to clarify who we are and why we are here? To do otherwise—to seek life advice from the enemy by pursuing a worldview other than that of our Maker—would be like telling a master artisan he did a terrible job at creating you, his masterpiece!

Today, let us take time to consult our Maker about to our

identity and purpose on Earth. Life flows more freely and fully when lived according to our identity and calling!

> For the gifts and the calling of God are irrevocable.

> — ROMANS 11:29

OCTOBER 28

"And You brought the rain"

We tend to grow comfortable in our lives as we become more mature. As we grow adept at walking in grace and are assured of who and of whose we are, we can fall into a moments of self-reliance. We call it maturity in Christ while actually walking in our own strength and abilities. But let's be reminded: *God* gave us our intellect. *God* gave us our abilities. *God* gave us our emotional giftings. Only One is responsible for any success we have in life — Father and those He uses to bless our lives. He brings the planting. He brings the rain. He causes the growth. He brings the harvest. We receive all the benefits.

Today, let us not forget this. Let us walk in gratitude.

> But I say to you, love your enemies and pray for those who persecute you, so that you may be sons of your Father who is in heaven; for He causes His sun to rise on the evil and the good, and sends rain on the righteous and the unrighteous.

> — MATTHEW 5:44-45

OCTOBER 29

"Lord of the Harvest, it's time once again to cast all the grain of my heart to the wind"

When we try to hold on to and keep a part of ourselves, we tend to fight against the One who *made* us! My time is *mine*. My work is *mine*. My talents are *mine*. We can become self-focused without even realizing it. But we are not here for our own glory and pleasure. We are here—we were created—for *His* glory and pleasure. And He chooses to bless others through us. My time is His time. My work is as unto Him. My talents are to be utilized for His Kingdom—whether anyone ever notices at all! I am His!

Let us walk in this attitude today, and stand back and marvel at the harvest He produces from such a life!

And He was saying to them, "The harvest is plentiful, but the laborers are few; therefore beseech the Lord of the harvest to send out laborers into His harvest."

— LUKE 10:2

OCTOBER 30

"So I throw my heart to the Wind"

What does it mean to throw one's heart to the wind? Being raised on a farm, I can actually remember a time when we harvested wheat and ground the grain into flour. Before we poured the wheat into the grinder, we threw the freshly harvested kernels into the air. Why? To allow the wind to bow out the debris—the chaff—that did not belong there, bringing greater purity and health to the final product. When we throw our hearts to the wind of the Spirit, He is able to blow out that which does not belong. And as we recognize the enemy's lies and replace them with truth, he is able to blow in the forgetfulness of God's forgiveness.

Throw your heart to the wind today—again and again!

Let those be ashamed and dishonored who seek my life;
Let those be turned back and humiliated who devise evil
against me.
Let them be like chaff before the wind,
With the angel of the Lord driving them on.

— PSALM 35:4-5

OCTOBER 31

"To blow out the chaff of my sin"

If impurities are allowed to remain in wheat, the bread made from it will be less than healthy. And less healthy means less life! Sin is like those impurities. But repentance is like throwing our hearts to the wind of God's Spirit. He blows in and reveals sin. We must allow that process to take place or our chaff will remain and our lives will be less than healthy in the end! And who wants that? Repentance is not a bad thing. God sees your sin and loves you anyway. If we truly believe this, what's the big deal of simply agreeing with God, confessing our sin, and moving on to greater purity and deeper life?

Today, try allowing God to blow away your chaff through confession.

Or do you think lightly of the riches of His kindness and tolerance and patience, not knowing that the kindness of God leads you to repentance?

— ROMANS 2:4

NOVEMBER

NOVEMBER 1

"I throw my heart to the Wind"

Not only do we throw our hearts to the Lord for cleansing, but we can throw our hearts to the Lord in joy, in gratitude, in worship, in honor, in thanksgiving for who He is and for all He has done and for all He is *going* to do!

Take time today to throw your heart to the wind of the Spirit and, out of sheer intimate gratitude, enjoy His presence. It will lift your heart and attitude and affect those around you in the process.

> I shall wash my hands in innocence,
>> And I will go about Your altar, O Lord,
>> That I may proclaim with the voice of thanksgiving

And declare all Your wonders.

— PSALM 26:6-7

NOVEMBER 2

"Blow through me again and again"

Being clean on the inside—having a clear conscience—affects every part of our existence. Being and feeling clean changes my perspective. Changing my perspective—seeing life from God's point of view—changes my attitudes and gives me grace to change my behavior. A kingdom perspective affects my entire being and allows me to be a better receiver of His love for me. God sees us right where we are and loves us there *anyway.* Why do we think we ever could (or should) hide from Him? Honest confession leaves me clean in every way, and that cleanliness affects all I touch on the outside. It makes me much more effective for the Kingdom!

Ask the Holy Spirit to blow through you again and again and again today. Live life in the clean conscience He affords you!

He sends forth His word and melts them;
He causes His wind to blow and the waters to flow.

— PSALM 147:18

NOVEMBER 3

"Father has planted a pure holy seed but by my own doing I've sown there a weed"

As a new creation in Christ, who I am is unchangeable. Once I am born again I cannot be un-born! So why do we continue to sin? We sin when we forget who and whose we are! It is when we allow ourselves to respond from the old ways of thinking—from the grave clothes that *used* to define us —that we allow the weeds of lies to take root in our minds. The remedy? Put off the lies and put on the truth of who we are! We never kill weeds by chopping the heads off. We kill weeds by eradicating the root system! So it is with the lies we believe.

Don't waste your time on the surface—get to the root of the lie and pull it out! Then replace the lie with what is true!

Finally, brethren, whatever is true, whatever is honorable, whatever is right, whatever is pure, whatever is lovely, whatever is of good repute, if there is any excellence and if anything worthy of praise, dwell on these things.

— PHILIPPIANS 4:8

NOVEMBER 4

"Sin, like a weed, sprouts again and again"

Having grown up on a farm, I understand the importance of getting to the root when it comes to eradicating weeds. If the root is not destroyed, the weed will always come back. It is that simple. And so it is with the lies we believe. We never eradicate those lies until we destroy them at the root! Like a hoe that is used to dig out the roots, use the Word of God to eradicate the lies that try to crowd your mind. Like a shot of Roundup that with one spray kills the roots of a weed, use the Word of God to kill those lies and then replace them with the truth of that Word.

Concerning the lies you have believed about yourself, put them off with the truth of who Father says you are. Deal with that and watch the garden of your mind spring to abundant life!

A man will not be established by wickedness,
But the root of the righteous will not be moved.

— PROVERBS 12:3

The wicked man desires the booty of evil men,
But the root of the righteous yields fruit.

— PROVERBS 12:12

NOVEMBER 5

"Can only be killed by a pure holy Wind"

We cannot defeat the enemy in our own strength; we are victorious over Him because of the blood of Jesus Christ! I never face the enemy alone—ever! I face the enemy with the Holy Spirit, with the Word of God, and with the authority afforded me by the power of the resurrection! Oh, yeah, there's one more thing I use to face the enemy—the powerful simple name of *Jesus!* Just the mention of His name sends the enemy running! But I must believe this is true to make it a reality in my life.

Face your enemy and His lies with all confidence today: confidence in the One who secured your victory on the cross and who He says you are!

Submit therefore to God. Resist the devil and he will flee from you.

— JAMES 4:7

NOVEMBER 6

"Holy Spirit, come"

Listen to the song "Holy Spirit, Come" from the album *The Worshipper's Collection Vol. 2.*

Holy Spirit, come,
We have need of Thee,
For You are the One
Who sets the thirsting free.
For we are dry,
But You are our supply
O come and fill us now.

Like a rushing wind,

Holy Spirit, Lord,
Come rushing in.

Holy Spirit, come
Without, within blow,
Like a rushing wind, blow.

We need Thee,
Come and help our eyes to see.
O come and fill us now.

When we worship God and use phrases like "Jesus, come" or "Holy Spirit, come into this place," we must remember that He is already here! What we are actually saying is, "Holy Spirit, come and be Yourself with and in me!" Where the Spirit of the Lord is, there is freedom, and freedom always begins with our honest confession of need. As believers, he is truly the Wind beneath our wings. He is the Comforter for our souls. He is the Powerful One who makes a way for us when we see no way or when we have no strength.

Today, spend time today confessing your need of the Holy Spirit. Trust Him to fill you as needed and let Him have His way with you.

But you will receive power when the Holy Spirit has come upon you; and you shall be My witnesses both in Jerusalem, and in all Judea and Samaria, and even to the remotest part of the earth.

— ACTS 1:8

NOVEMBER 7

"We have need of Thee"

We do not get the help we need if we never even admit we have a need! To resist help—due to pride or fear of what others might think—would be foolish. To not ask for help or admit one's need is like going to a doctor with a life-threatening wound but refusing to allow the doctor to treat it because of what someone might think! That would be foolish, yet we do that very thing with the Lord far too often.

Today, let us cut off pride and put the fear of man under our feet by simply admitting our need for Jesus. Do you need provision, wisdom, healing, friends, hope today? Tell Father, and believe and receive whatever He gives you.

> You lust and do not have; so you commit murder. You are envious and cannot obtain; so you fight and quarrel. You do not have because you do not ask.
>
> — JAMES 4:2

NOVEMBER 8

"For You are the One who sets the thirsty free"

When I am thirsty my body tells me in no uncertain terms "give me water!" I can try and quench my thirst with a cracker or slice of bread, but that wouldn't work. I could try and quench my thirst with a new car or pleasurable experience, but

I would still be thirsty. The only thing that truly quenches my thirst is that which was meant to satisfy it—water! When we try to satisfy our spiritual, physical, or emotional needs with anything other than that which truly quenches them, we still thirst!

Let us remember this today and seek the Living Water of intimacy with Christ, which truly satisfies our need.

He who believes in Me, as the Scripture said, "From his innermost being will flow rivers of living water."

— JOHN 7:38

~

NOVEMBER 9

"We are dry but You are our Supply"

It is when we go through dry times that we truly appreciate the rain. It is when we go through the heat of summer that we truly appreciate plunging into a cool deep pool. It is when we go through the trials of life that we truly appreciate the presence and power and grace of God. After we have experienced those times of refreshing, we want to keep coming back, and that is good and right and natural!

Let us spend time plunging into, drinking of, and acknowledging the presence of God with us and in us today. Keep coming back as often as desired, as often as necessary!

Therefore repent and return, so that your sins may be wiped

away, in order that times of refreshing may come from the presence of the Lord.

— ACTS 3:19

NOVEMBER 10

"Oh, come and fill us now"

When we hunger and thirst after God—when we understand that apart from Him we cannot survive—we understand our need to be filled with the Holy Spirit. We, as new creations, are temples of the Holy Spirit—His dwelling place. At the same time, our greatest strength is mere weakness when compared to the power of the Holy Spirit. When do we need to be filled? At all times, I say! When I am sad, I need Him. When I am angry, I need His power to flow through me. When I am bewildered with making the right decision, I need His powerful wisdom. When I am joyful, I still need Him to be the object of my joy, yet at the same time, the reason for my joy! Simply put—I just need Him, like I need food and water and the air I breathe.

He will fill us if we will ask. Ask Him.

Do you not know that you are a temple of God and that the Spirit of God dwells in you?

— 1 CORINTHIANS 3:16

"Like a rushing wind, Holy Spirit"

There is power in the wind even though we cannot see it. We see evidence of the wind's power as a windmill turns and produces electricity, as a sail fills and propels a boat, as a leaf blower cleans away debris on a sidewalk. Though as we cannot see the Holy Spirit, we still see evidence of His power when we face a difficult decision and suddenly have an impression of the way to go, or when we avoid a conflict but suddenly gain the peace and love required to deal with the issue face to face!

Be filled with the Holy Spirit today, and let His wind blow right through you.

When the day of Pentecost had come, they were all together in one place. And suddenly there came from heaven a noise like a violent rushing wind, and it filled the whole house where they were sitting. And there appeared to them tongues as of fire distributing themselves, and they rested on each one of them. And they were all filled with the Holy Spirit and began to speak with other tongues, as the Spirit was giving them utterance.

— ACTS 2:1-4

NOVEMBER 12

"Lord, come rushing in, Holy Spirit"

Very often, we are so overwhelmed by the life's circumstances that we feel as if we are swimming against a raging
flood. Who do you suppose wants us to feel that way? The
enemy! Let's get a Kingdom point of view on this matter. If we
see a flood coming against us, I believe the King sees a deluge
of opportunities to receive His grace! The Spirit of God longs
to come in like a raging flood and bolster and ravish us with
grace!

Turn the tables on the enemy today and see life from the
King's point of view. Go with *His* flow!

So they will fear the name of the Lord from the west
> And His glory from the rising of the sun,
> For He will come like a rushing stream
> Which the wind of the Lord drives.

— ISAIAH 59:19

NOVEMBER 13

"Come without, within"

Do we need the Lord only on the surface of our lives or do
we need the power of the Holy Spirit in every nook and
cranny? I say we need Him in every intimate detail of life! Let
us practice being filled with the Holy Spirit. Let us ask Him to

bear forth the fruit of the Spirit in our lives—the evidence in our very being that He is filling and empowering us for Kingdom work.

Ask and believe and receive, and enjoy the fruit!

> But the fruit of the Spirit is love, joy, peace, patience, kindness, goodness, faithfulness, gentleness, self-control; against such things there is no law.

— GALATIANS 5:22-23

NOVEMBER 14

"Blow! Like a rushing wind, blow"

When I mow my driveway, I often look back to see the entire surface covered with grass clippings, but after only a few minutes of allowing the wind to blow, I look back and see those clippings are nowhere to be found! That is the power of the wind and a wonderful picture of the power of the Holy Spirit —He blows into our wounded, weary, worried souls and clears the clippings of our pain! Seeing life from the perspective of the Holy Spirit allows Him to blow through our minds and purify our thoughts! That is truly having one's mind blown!

Let Him blow your mind in a holy way today! Ask Him to allow you to think His thoughts!

> But just as it is written, "Things which eye has not seen and ear has not heard, and which have not entered the heart of man, all that God has prepared for those who love him."

— 1 CORINTHIANS 2:9

NOVEMBER 15

"We need Thee"

Do you need air in order to stay alive? Do you need food and water in order to continue your physical existence? Then why do we think we can survive without the spiritual necessities of an abundant life? No matter how healthy or mature I become as a new creation, my foundational belief is that I need Him desperately or I *will not survive!* This foundational way of thinking keeps my soul ever-ready, always expectant, to hear from and rely upon the power of the Holy Spirit.

Live like you need Him today.
>The Spirit of God has made me,
>And the breath of the Almighty gives me life.

— JOB 33:4

NOVEMBER 16

"Come and help our eyes to see"

Even when I am at my most spiritually sensitive — very aware of the spiritual reality of my existence — I see through a glass dimly. In order to see and discern, I must rely on the power of the Holy Spirit to infuse my soul and lead me in power and wisdom and grace. When we acknowledge our need for God's power, He pours out His power upon us. It is a grand thing to see even the most mundane thing from the King's point of view.

Spend time today acknowledging your need for greater wisdom and clarity of vision from the Spirit's point of view.

My eyes are continually toward the Lord,
For He will pluck my feet out of the net.

— PSALM 25:15

NOVEMBER 17

"Oh, come and fill us now!"

When do we need to be filled with the power of the Holy Spirit? Always! When I am sad, I need His powerful infilling to encourage my soul. When I am angry, I need His powerful peace to invade my angry places. When I am bewildered or overwhelmed with life, I need Him to fill me with His powerful wisdom and grace to endure. There is no wrong time to be filled. There is no inconvenient time to be filled. Quite the contrary—we need to constantly be filled with His Holy Spirit!

Take time to ask Him to fill you to overflowing *right now!*

For this reason I bow my knees before the Father, from whom every family in heaven and on earth derives its name, that He would grant you, according to the riches of His glory, to be strengthened with power through His Spirit in the inner man, so that Christ may dwell in your hearts through faith; and that you, being rooted and grounded in love, may be able to comprehend with all the saints what is the breadth and length and height and depth, and to know the love of Christ which surpasses knowledge, that you may be filled up to all the fullness of God.

— EPHESIANS 3:14-19

NOVEMBER 18

"You are my God"

Listen to the song "You Are My God" from the album *The Worshipper's Collection Vol. 2.*

You are my God. I am Your servant.
Father of mine, I am your child.
You are my God. I Your creation.
I find my joy here in Your smile.

You are my light when I'm in darkness.
You are my Rock when stormy winds fly.
You are my strength when I am weakest.
You are my life when I would die.
You are my God. I Your creation.
I find my joy here in Your smile.

You are my Lord. I bow before You.
You are my King. In honor I stand.
I am Your bride. You are the bridegroom.
I long for the day when You take my hand!

You are the Truth when the enemy's lying.
You are my Way when I cannot see.
You are my Joy when sorrow brings crying.
You are my Hope when the world rejects me.
I am Your bride. You are the bridegroom.
I long for the day when You take my hand!

To acknowledge that "God is God and I am not" is a major step toward freedom and wholeness and healing and hope! We become so accustomed to making our own way through life that we assume *we* have everything to do with our success. Nothing could be further from the truth. Life is much less burdensome and fretful when we remember to step down from the throne of our heart and allow the Lord to sit there! Without His grace, I cannot bear my own burdens. Apart from His wisdom, I cannot make the best decisions. Ultimately, all my success can be attributed directly to the Lord.

"He is God. I am not!" Make this statement to yourself today, meditate on it, and apply it to your life.

For You are great and do wondrous deeds;
You alone are God.

— PSALM 86:10

NOVEMBER 19

"I am your servant"

What is a servant? One who serves another. True service requires the laying down of life. When I place the needs of others as more important than my own I am transported into the realm of Kingdom thinking—servant thinking—and life is made much simpler. I am not here for my own glory or pleasure but for His. Jesus came to serve, I am a new creation and joint-heir with Him in that work, therefore, I am a servant!

Today, let us take time to serve those around us, whether we receive recognition for those acts of service or not.

> But it is not this way among you, but whoever wishes to become great among you shall be your servant; and whoever wishes to be first among you shall be slave of all. For even the Son of Man did not come to be served, but to serve, and to give His life a ransom for many.

> — MARK 10:43-45

~

NOVEMBER 20

"Father of mine, I am Your child"

If we are to walk in victory as overcomers, understanding our identity is *everything!* When we walk in insecurity concerning our identity, the enemy and his lies have power over our thoughts. My victory is in knowing who I am and whose I am. My life has been purchased by the blood of Jesus which means I am forgiven, washed, redeemed, and granted a new identity in Christ! I am a child of the Most High God which means that, as a joint-heir with Christ, I have been granted the keys to the Kingdom of God! All that is available to Jesus is available to *me!*

This day, let us take advantage of this reality and walk in the assurance of whose and of who we are!

My beloved is mine, and I am his.

— SONG OF SONGS 2:16A

NOVEMBER 21

"You are my God. I, your creation"

I am adamant about this: understanding my identity in Christ is the key to my victory in this life. And the most wonderful part about this is that this identity is best understood and realized *as* I walk in relationship with my God! He is the Creator; I am the *new* creation! All my old has passed away because He has chosen to make all things new, by virtue of the new covenant of the blood of Christ! If I do not walk in the relationship afforded me, I never get to experience any of the benefits.

Walk boldly in your true identity in Christ today and receive all the benefits this relationship affords you!

For in Him we live and move and exist, as even some of your own poets have said, "For we also are His children."

— ACTS 17:28

"I find my joy here in Your smile"

We need to understand that not only does our God *love* us, He *likes* us as well—and likes just being with us! If we believe God loves us based on our performance, we never realize the depth of relationship available to us! As a parent smiles at the mere thought of their child, how much more is our heavenly Father capable of loving and smiling down upon us? Don't beat yourself up feeling you need to perform for God's acceptance or approval. That way of thinking plays right into the enemy's hands. Accept His love and affirmation simply because it is freely offered to you. In that moment, your attitude will change. Then, performance will come as a *result* of the depth of love you have experienced!

Today, stop striving to perform for God's love. Simply accept it, and see how your actions change.

We have come to know and have believed the love which God has for us. God is love, and the one who abides in love abides in God, and God abides in him.

— 1 JOHN 4:16

"You are my Light when I'm in darkness"

Even if the Lord has brought us through years of growth

and maturity, we still go through times of darkness. When I was a child and the lights went out in a storm, fear immediately invaded my mind. But as I grew and matured, I responded less fearfully when the lights would flicker and go out. Due to my years of maturity, I knew several things that calmed my fear. I knew the storm would pass. I knew the power would come back on. I knew just where the obstacles in my home were, even if I could not see them. In our spiritual walk, it is no different. As we grow in maturity, we realize that, just because there are seasons of darkness does not mean the Light has stopped shining. Our God is constant—in darkness and in light. We can trust Him to be our Light.

What areas of darkness do you face today? Where is God in that darkness? Trust Him there.

For you were formerly darkness, but now you are Light in the Lord; walk as children of Light.

— EPHESIANS 5:8

NOVEMBER 24

"You are my Rock when stormy winds fly"

When the foundation on which we stand crumbles beneath us, we fall. Why do we so often insist on being our own foundation? It is the wise man or woman who knows that the house built on solid ground withstands the storms of life. In this life we face many storms, enough to drive us mad at times. Yet, it is through weathering the storm that we grow less fearful of the next one—because we know we do not weather it alone. It is when we choose to stand firmly on the Solid Rock, regardless of our circumstances, that the storms of life have the least effect upon our souls. In fact, a storm weathered on the foundation of Jesus Christ becomes a *growing* experience from which we learn to receive and operate in more grace!

Stand on the Foundation today—don't budge—and weather the next storm.

> For in the day of trouble He will conceal me in His tabernacle;
>> In the secret place of His tent He will hide me;
>> He will lift me up on a rock.

> — PSALM 27:5

NOVEMBER 25

"You are my Strength when I am weakened"

Trying times and circumstances make us weary on this journey of life. When is the last time you gave yourself permission to spend the day doing nothing? Every so often, I realize I have not given my soul a chance to breathe—frequently in the name of ministry—and finally, near the brink of exhaustion, I put a stop to the madness. One of the most spiritual things I can do is rest in Jesus and refresh my soul, body, mind, and emotions. But I can only do that if I lay down my need to perform for the approval of others.

Assess your life right now. Do you need a break? What can you do to cease the striving, even for ten minutes, and refresh your soul? Ask the Holy Spirit to guide you in this matter and trust Him to fill you to overflowing.

Cease striving and know that I am God;
I will be exalted among the nations, I will be exalted in the earth.

— PSALM 46:10

NOVEMBER 26

"You are my Life when I would die"

God is in control no matter what, even if we feel out of control! We must view life from the Kingdom point of view. From that perspective we can see hope where there is despair, we can see joy where there is sorrow, we can see peace where there is chaos, and we can see life where there is death. We realize our true identities as new creations when we completely trust in and rest upon the person of the Lord Jesus Christ and the power of the Holy Spirit. Before Christ we saw only hopelessness, but *in* Christ we know hope—in any circumstance!

Get to the King's point of view today and *live* there!

We know that we have passed out of death into life, because we love the brethren. He who does not love abides in death.

— 1 JOHN 3:14

NOVEMBER 27

"You are my Lord - I bow before You"

We must choose daily who we will serve. We can serve ourselves, or we can serve the enemy, or we can serve God and others. Guess which way brings peace, joy, contentment, fulfillment, and purpose? When, in the name of Jesus, we serve others, we effectively bow our heart to our King. As we serve, we testify to the power of our God, whether those we serve realize it or not. By bowing our knees in service to God and others, we submit to the divine power of Jesus Christ and receive bold empowering grace to fulfill any task, regardless of compensation or notice. By taking our eyes off of own needs and selves, we travel far in understanding our identities and callings in Christ.

Today, bow before Him in service to those around you.

Come, let us worship and bow down,
Let us kneel before the Lord our Maker.

— PSALM 95:6

NOVEMBER 28

"You are my King - In honor I stand"

In most cultures, it is customary to stand in honor when a king or queen enters the room. Likewise, there are a variety of ways we can stand to honor the Lord. We can exalt Him in corporate worship. We can build a house to shelter a needy family. We can do any number of things, but what will we do when society tells us we must bow our knee to some other god? Will we stand in honor to the true God or will we sheepishly bow the knee in fear of man? As our culture slides down the slippery slope of humanism, we will all be called to make a stand one way or another. In that moment, God has grace for you and will meet you there. I have already decided that if my testimony becomes regarded as hate speech, I will simply have a prison ministry—from the inside! God will meet me, even there, with His amazing grace and purpose.

What would you do?

> No one can serve two masters; for either he will hate the one and love the other, or he will be devoted to one and despise the other. You cannot serve God and wealth.
>
> — MATTHEW 6:24

NOVEMBER 29

"I am Your bride"

What does it mean for us to be called the Bride of Christ? As a man, it is more difficult to understand, but as I think about my wife anticipating marriage during our engagement, I get a glimpse of what this might mean. She had great expectations for our union. She was beyond excited at the mention of spending the rest of her life with me. She was more than willing to wait for me, yet gave herself completely and fully to me after our wedding. I remember how much it meant to be so honored by her—the way she spoke to others about me, the way she looked at me, the way she touched me. If we could translate those perceptions to our relationship with Christ, it would dramatically increase our power to overcome, because such intimate passion leads to power and life.

Today, spend time imagining yourself as the Bride of Christ and let this revolutionize your walk with Him!

The Spirit and the bride say, "Come." And let the one who hears say, "Come." And let the one who is thirsty come; let the one who wishes take the water of life without cost.

— REVELATION 22:17

NOVEMBER 30

"You are the Bridegroom"

In understanding that we are the Bride of Christ, we must also consider what it means for Christ to be our Bride*groom*. Just as my wife waited for our wedding day with great anticipation and celebration, we must view our Bridegroom in that same manner—trusting He indeed is coming for us, placing our hope in Him, expecting nothing but the finest when the wedding feast is celebrated. Just as an engaged couple spends time getting to know one another, spending time getting to know Him breeds life and peace and joy and hope in the bride of Christ!

Meditate today on what it means for Christ to be *your* Bridegroom. How should you prepare to greet Him? What would you like to say to Him? What can He do to help you prepare for the wedding? Allow the Holy Spirit to show you facets of the Bridegroom you gave no thought to before now.

> He who has the bride is the bridegroom; but the friend of the
> bridegroom, who stands and hears him, rejoices greatly
> because of the bridegroom's voice. So this joy of mine has
> been made full. He must increase, but I must decrease. He
> who comes from above is above all, he who is of the earth is
> from the earth and speaks of the earth. He who comes from
> heaven is above all.

— JOHN 3:29-31

DECEMBER

DECEMBER 1

"I long for the day when You take my hand"

Knowing Jesus intimately is a matter of faith. As a new creation, I experience His creativity and respond to Him with creativity of my own. As His sheep, I experience His guidance as Shepherd and respond to Him by following wherever He leads. In the process, I find green pastures of sustenance, I drink deeply of pure Living Water, my wounds are cared for and healed, and a feast of triumph is set before me in the midst of my enemies! That's all as a result of the faith God has granted me! I can only imagine what it will be like when I finally take His hand!

Ponder these things today: life with Him here and life with Him in eternity!

For now we see in a mirror dimly, but then face to face; now
I know in part, but then I will know fully just as I also have
been fully known.

— 1 CORINTHIANS 13:12

DECEMBER 2

"You are my Truth when the enemy's lying"

The enemy lives to deceive us. When we settle that truth, understanding the true battle and weapons necessary to defeat our enemy become more and more clear. The battleground of our life is our *mind*. And the weapons of our warfare are myriad! The Word of God. The power of the Holy Spirit. The power of praise and worship. The body of Christ standing with us. The shield of faith. The presence of God! When we learn to accept our identity in Christ we effectively thwart the enemy's greatest plan of all!

Walk as one who knows who and whose they are today. Use that weapon often and boldly!

For though we walk in the flesh, we do not war according to
the flesh, for the weapons of our warfare are not of the flesh,
but divinely powerful for the destruction of fortresses.

— 2 CORINTHIANS 10:3-4

DECEMBER 3

"You are my Way when I cannot see"

Our enemy operates most effectively in darkness, but he also disguises himself as an angel of light! We must be ever vigilant in guarding our hearts. Anything contrary to God's nature and our nature as new creations can be used as a weapon against us. Do not be deceived by the subtle half-truths of the world that disguise themselves as messengers of compassion and tolerance. True love requires sacrifice rather than compromising our identity. Stand for who you. Stand for whose you are. And apologize for neither.

Today, bathe your life in love and respond to those who curse you with blessing, and watch the Lord bring honor to your life.

> But what I am doing I will continue to do, so that I may cut off opportunity from those who desire an opportunity to be regarded just as we are in the matter about which they are boasting. For such men are false apostles, deceitful workers, disguising themselves as apostles of Christ. No wonder, for even Satan disguises himself as an angel of light. Therefore it is not surprising if his servants also disguise themselves as servants of righteousness, whose end will be according to their deeds.

— 2 CORINTHIANS 11:12-15

DECEMBER 4

"You are my joy when sorrow brings crying"

I had a revelation this morning. It was one I've had several times in my life, but this time seemed different. That revelation? God knows my needs and He is in control, so why do I worry? We often think things like, "If I only had a surplus of cash, I would be all right," or "If I could just gain enough notoriety and fame, I would have it made," or "If I could just feel a certain way, life would be easier." Since when does money or fame or even the way I feel dictate my life? Only if I choose to not see from a Kingdom perspective.

Take a look at your life today and see if there are any areas you are viewing from the wrong vantage point. Make the necessary adjustments and move on into deeper life.

> O Lord, in Your strength the king will be glad,
> And in Your salvation how greatly he will rejoice!
>
> — PSALM 21:1

DECEMBER 5

"You are my Hope when the world rejects me"

As long as we follow Jesus we will walk in the fellowship of His suffering. The enemy of God will see to that! But the Good News is our inevitable victory! We win no matter what! When we live our lives as victors rather than as victims, we set ourselves up for success rather than settling for defeat before the battle has even begun! My hope is not in what people think of me. My hope is not in whether or not the world receives me or rejects me. My hope is not in earthly success. My hope is assured in my relationship with Jesus Christ! I walk with Him through *whatever* circumstance life brings my way, and He blesses me and receives glory and honor in the process. Others will long to know my God by virtue of the love that emanates from him through me!

Walk in this hope today!

> He put a new song in my mouth, a song of praise to our God;
> Many will see and fear
> And will trust in the Lord.

— PSALM 40:3

DECEMBER 6

"I am Your bride. You are the Bridegroom. I long for the day when You take my hand"

I am His bride. Jesus is my Bridegroom. Like a bride that anticipates life with her husband, I long for deeper fellowship and intimacy with my God! Spend time today simply dreaming of ways you would love to experience intimacy with God. Tell Him your desires. Trust your heart to Him and welcome Him. Be a good receiver of all the blessings He wants to pour out on you. Walk in wonder and gratitude at what He reveals to you. Let these new discoveries and depths of His love spur you on to even deeper and greater levels of knowing Him in *this* life!

But whatever things were gain to me, those things I have counted as loss for the sake of Christ. More than that, I count all things to be loss in view of the surpassing value of knowing Christ Jesus my Lord, for whom I have suffered the loss of all things, and count them but rubbish so that I may gain Christ, and may be found in Him, not having a righteousness of my own derived from the Law, but that which is through faith in Christ, the righteousness which comes from God on the basis of faith, that I may know Him and the power of His resurrection and the fellowship of His sufferings, being conformed to His death.

— PHILIPPIANS 3:7-10

DECEMBER 7

"Oh, Lord, I will sing to You for You give life to me"

Listen to the song "I Delight In You" from the album *The Worshipper's Collection Vol. 2.*

Oh Lord, I will sing to You, for You give life to me.
My heart, I gladly give to You the way You give Your heart
    to me.
Oh Lord, You've been good to me through heartache, pain and
    trial.
Your love has freed this child to be, delighted, resting in Your
    smile.

Oh Lord, I delight in You for I know that You take delight
    in me.

Oh Lord, I delight in You.
Where You go I'll follow You willingly.
Oh Lord, I delight in You for You gave Your life just to set me
*   free to delight in You.*
You delight in me.

My child, I will sing to you for you bring joy to Me!
Oh, and my heart takes great delight in you
And the way you give your heart to me!

My child, I delight in you for I know that you take delight
*   in me!*
Oh, My child I delight in you and I'll always be watching you
*   lovingly!*
Because, My child I delight in you and I gave my life just to set
*   you free*
To delight in Me and I delight in you!
Child, I delight in You! (You're my precious Father!)

You are My son! (Oh, I love You!)
You are My pride and joy! (Father, I love You!)
I love you! (Oh, I delight in You! I delight in You!)
I love You! I love You! (Father, I love you)
I love you! I do! (I love you!)

Why are you here? Because someone spoke you into existence and used your parents as the earthly delivery system! When we realize this foundational truth and believe that we are destined (called and appointed) to be sons and daughters of the Most High God, we are more prepared to traverse this life and its many trials.

Let us spend time today pondering the far-reaching effects

and benefits this truth holds for new creations. Let the things the Holy Spirit reveals to you permeate the way you make choices today, and walk in the joy of the life that is revealed to you!

> For You formed my inward parts;
>> You wove me in my mother's womb.
> I will give thanks to You, for I am fearfully and wonderfully made;
>> Wonderful are Your works,
>> And my soul knows it very well.

> — PSALM 139:13-14

DECEMBER 8

"My heart I gladly give to You the way You give Your heart to me"

Jesus freely gave everything He was and had to purchase you and make you His own. He left the riches and glory of Heaven because He wanted *you!* That means you do not have to perform for His love and acceptance. You already *have* it! He gave Himself completely to you in every way possible. It is when we understand and embrace this truth that we stop performing to *gain* His love and begin performing out of the sheer joy of being so completely loved *by* Him!

Enjoy today as you contemplate all the ramifications of this truth in your life.

> Willingly I will sacrifice to You;

I will give thanks to Your name, O Lord, for it is good.

— PSALM 54:6

He who did not spare His own Son, but delivered Him over for us all, how will He not also with Him freely give us all things?

— ROMANS 8:32

DECEMBER 9

"Oh, Lord, You've been good to me through heartache, pain, and trial"

We often say God is good but somewhere in the back of our minds we still think "except when bad things happened to me." What I have discovered is that, even the bad things that have happened to me—whether by my own foolishness or otherwise —God will use for my good and His glory *if* I bring them to Him in honesty!

Take time to look back and see how He has used heartache, pain, or trials to bring about something good for you. Then, inventory your current trials and ask Him to do the same. And give Him thanks in all things.

Whoever speaks, is to do so as one who is speaking the utterances of God; whoever serves is to do so as one who is serving by the strength which God supplies; so that in all things God may be glorified through Jesus Christ, to whom belongs the glory and dominion forever and ever. Amen.

Beloved, do not be surprised at the fiery ordeal among

you, which comes upon you for your testing, as though some strange thing were happening to you; but to the degree that you share the sufferings of Christ, keep on rejoicing, so that also at the revelation of His glory you may rejoice with exultation.

— 1 PETER 4:11-13

DECEMBER 10

"Oh, but Your love has freed this child to be delighted, resting in Your smile"

Once, I was in bondage to sin and an identity that reeked of death. But Jesus found me in my lostness and rescued me, redeeming me from the curse of the Law! I no longer have to perform to be good and righteous. Now, that is my nature as a new creation! This revelation has freed me to walk in joy despite my circumstances. It has given me reason not to despair, though darkness descend upon me for a season. Through every trial and in any circumstance I can freely delight and bask in the peaceful light of His presence!

Delight in Him today at the realization of His delight in *you*!

When my anxious thoughts multiply within me,
Your consolations delight my soul.

— PSALM 94:19

DECEMBER 11

"Oh, Lord I delight in You for I know that You take delight in me"

Recently, my wife and I had the opportunity to spend several nights being with our entire brood. This is not an easy task since most of our nine children are now on their own and scattered from Sydney, Australia to Kandern, Germany! As we sat in their midst, our children told many stories of their young years and how they delighted in our family. I cried and I laughed at the sheer joy of just *being* with my children, and it dawned on me: if I take this much joy in simply being with my children, how much more delight does our heavenly Father take in being with *His* children?!

Delight in God's delight and rest in His smile.

The Lord your God is in your midst,
  A victorious warrior.
  He will exult over you with joy,
  He will be quiet in His love,
  He will rejoice over you with shouts of joy.

— ZEPHANIAH 3:17

DECEMBER 12

"Oh, Lord, I delight in You"

What things or activities bring you the most joy in life?

Being with your spouse? Playing with your children or grand-children? Golf? Sewing? Board games? Collecting memora-bilia? The greatest delight I know is when I am sharing an activity with someone I love! I love scuba diving and have done a solo dive, but I didn't get to experience my discoveries with anyone. My family and friends weren't able to fully understand my joy because they had not been there *with* me. Delight comes when life is shared and lived with those we love.

Today, take time to enjoy someone else's company and delight in them.

Be devoted to one another in brotherly love; give preference to one another in honor.

— ROMANS 12:10

DECEMBER 13

"Where You go I'll follow You willingly"

When I lived under the law of performance, I fought the will of God. But when I realized the New Covenant of God's grace, I no longer felt the need to perform for His acceptance. This, in turn, freed me to perform out of the sheer joy of being loved so completely. I no longer perform to *be* loved. I now perform because I *am* loved! That is a level of trust every human heart longs for. If He loves me, He wants only what is best for me. Since I can trust Him and His love, I can follow Him fully and completely!

In what areas do you lack trust today? Ask the Lord to reveal any areas of performance-based identity and allow Him to rip them away. Then, simply begin to walk in freedom and trust!

Then Jesus said to His disciples, "If anyone wishes to come after Me, he must deny himself, and take up his cross and follow Me. For whoever wishes to save his life will lose it; but whoever loses his life for My sake will find it."

— MATTHEW 16:24-25

DECEMBER 14

"Oh, Lord, I delight in You"

To delight in something is to take great joy or pleasure in that thing. As new creations, we are designed for delighting in the Lord and in receiving His delight in us. But if we believe we do not measure up to His standards or are somehow unworthy of His delight, we never get to fully experience it! The truth is that in our sin we never could measure up to His standards and were not worthy of His delight. *But,* He wanted us to walk in relationship with Him, and the shed blood of Jesus Christ sealed our eternal fate. We could never have earned His approval or cleansing or delight, but by virtue of the blood of Jesus, we have His approval, cleansing, and delight!

Delight in this reality today!

When my anxious thoughts multiply within me,
  Your consolations delight my soul.

— PSALM 94:19

DECEMBER 15

"For You gave Your life just to set me free to delight in You"

Jesus sacrificed Himself to secure our freedom from performance even though He knew many of us would reject His sacrificial love. In a sense, it was His delight—His joy and pleasure—to express His love in the laying down of His life. He wanted us that much! His delight is in knowing us relationally. As He delights in us, we delight in Him! That's the goal!

Take time to refresh your soul by delighting in the Lord in worship today, and find fulfillment as you receive His delight for you!

Fixing our eyes on Jesus, the author and perfecter of faith, who for the joy set before Him endured the cross, despising the shame, and has sat down at the right hand of the throne of God.

— HEBREWS 12:2

DECEMBER 16

"You delight in me"

Our Father delights in us, but the enemy desires to keep us from understanding and living in this reality. Why do you think he spends so much time trying to make you and I feel so inadequate and unworthy and defeated? He wants to keep us from the abundance of life and ultimate victory that are ours as new creations! Our Father not only *loves* us, but He *likes* us as well!

Today, spend time focusing on the ways God loves you and likes you. Then, spend time thanking Him by telling Him how much you love and like Him!

> You will make known to me the path of life;
>> In Your presence is fullness of joy;
>> In Your right hand there are pleasures forever.

> — PSALM 16:11

DECEMBER 17

"My child, I will sing to you for you bring joy to me"

When we sing to God in praise, we effectively put a shield of protection around our minds. Think about it. To sing to God requires our entire being. We must engage our minds. We must engage our bodies. We must engage even our emotions and attitudes. By praising God in song, we give the enemy *no place at all* to plant his devious seeds of deception!

Be free today! Worship your God in song!!!

> Break forth, shout joyfully together,
>> You waste places of Jerusalem;
>> For the Lord has comforted His people,
>> He has redeemed Jerusalem.

> — ISAIAH 52:9

DECEMBER 18

"My heart takes great delight in You and the way you give your heart to Me"

I have a bit of experience relating to my nine children as a father. I have no favorites, but I must admit, when a child expresses gratitude or expresses love by hugging me or leaning on my shoulder, I melt into emotional oneness with them. And I am simply an *earthly* father! How much more does our Heavenly Father respond when we lean into Him with a grateful heart?

Spend time thanking God today for the simple fact of His dear presence in your life. Lay your head on His shoulder and simply *be* with Him. He'll lean back into you.

Just as a father has compassion on his children,
So the Lord has compassion on those who fear Him.

— PSALM 103:13

DECEMBER 19

"My child, I delight in you for I know that you take delight in me"

When one of my children expresses love for me — whether in a touch, a kind word of thanks, or a simple shared laugh — my hearts melts in sheer joy. I say this often but it bears hearing again and again: I feel this way as an earthly father, so how much more is our heavenly Father capable of delighting in *us?!*

Today, I challenge you to see if what I share is not true. Spend time today delighting in His delight over you. Let Him love you.

> For God so loved the world, that He gave His only begotten Son, that whoever believes in Him shall not perish, but have eternal life.
>
> — JOHN 3:16

DECEMBER 20

"My child, I delight in you"

Let us embark on an all-day exercise today. Ask the Holy Spirit to show you all the ways Father delights in you. From the way you are physically made to the intricacies of your personality. From the family you were born into to the dreams and visions He has placed within you. See from the King's perspective just how much He delights in you. See this as a meditation on who you are in Christ and what it means to belong to Him.

> If you then, being evil, know how to give good gifts to your children, how much more will your Father who is in heaven give what is good to those who ask Him!
>
> — MATTHEW 7:11

DECEMBER 21

"My child, I delight in you and I'll always be watching You! Loving You!"

Our hope cannot be found in anything other than the One who made us. Money can be gone in a flash. People can be gone in an instant. Fame is fleeting. Possessions are not able to walk in relationship with us. Even our own physical health is nothing to place our hope in. There is only one sure place to place our hope—only one sure Foundation—and that is in Jesus. He is always here. He is always delighting in us. He is watching over us even when we disregard Him. He *loves* us!

Today, remind your soul of this truth and delight in it.

In peace I will both lie down and sleep,
For You alone, O Lord, make me to dwell in safety.

— PSALM 4:8

DECEMBER 22

"Because My child, I delight in You and I gave My life just to set You free"

Why do we go through times when we think God does not love us or like us? I think it is because we believe the subtle lies of the enemy, and because the enemy delights in trying to get us to focus on performance rather than grace. Even when we were at our worst in sin, He still willingly died for you and I because He *wanted* us! And He wanted relationship with us because He loved us! I love and like being with my children. Just because they do something that disappoints me doesn't mean I no longer love or like them, and I am an *earthly father!* How much more capable is our *heavenly Father* of loving us for who we are?

Dwell on this truth today.

But God demonstrates His own love toward us, in that while we were yet sinners, Christ died for us.

— ROMANS 5:8

DECEMBER 23

"To delight in Me as I delight in You"

Today, let us practice loving God in this way: to the degree that you have experienced His love, try to love Him back with the same degree of passion. To the degree that you have experienced His delight for you, spend time delighting passionately in Him. How could this be anything but a blessing? Be blessed today!

Delight yourself in the Lord;
    And He will give you the desires of your heart.

— PSALM 37:4

DECEMBER 24

"How can I keep silent when my Father has set me free?"

Listen to the song "I Will Celebrate The Goodness Of The Lord" from the album *The Worshipper's Collection Vol. 2.*

How can I keep silent when my Father has set me free?
I cannot keep silent when He's lavished boundless love on me.
So let the world knock me down, and try to steal it.
A heart of joy cannot be bound! They can't conceal it!

O, I will celebrate the goodness of the Lord!
He gave His life for me, yet He keeps giving more!
O Lord, I celebrate Your goodness!
You are good, Lord!
I will celebrate the goodness of the King,
For giving me new life, reason to live and sing!
O Lord, I celebrate your goodness, your goodness!

Think of Paul and Silas bound in prison, in lock and chain.
We, like Paul and Silas, have a joy that cannot be contained!
So let the world knock me down, my flesh restrain it,
My heart cannot be bound! I'll still proclaim it!

Have you ever received such good news that you simply could not keep yourself from sharing it with others? When each of my children were born, I was so excited that I would share the good news with even the complete strangers I encountered! As I write this devotion, I am going through a time when the enemy is trying to quiet me from sharing the truth of my freedom. Any way you look at it, persecution is not fun. Yet, what keeps me proclaiming is the Good News of how much Father loves us. This makes me want to share my redemption with others who find themselves in bondage—even complete strangers! How could I keep silent?

How can you share your good news today both practically and in attitude? Be prepared to share the excitement!

> You have turned for me my mourning into dancing;
> You have loosed my sackcloth and girded me with gladness,
> That my soul may sing praise to You and not be silent.
> O Lord my God, I will give thanks to You forever.
>
> — PSALM 30:11-12

DECEMBER 25

"I cannot keep silent when He's lavished boundless love on me"

To the degree that I have been loved by God and have found healing and deliverance in the process, I get to delight in watching others hear of my joy and desire it for themselves! This is a very natural thing. I do not have to stand on a street corner and shout it out. I can live my life in honest transparency and it will be a public statement to the boundless love of God that has been lavished upon me.

Ask the Holy Spirit how you can speak loudly without saying a word today.

In Him we have redemption through His blood, the

forgiveness of our trespasses, according to the riches of His grace which He lavished on us.

— EPHESIANS 1:7-8A

DECEMBER 26

"So let the world knock me down and try to steal it"

As we serve God and walk in the righteous calling of our new identity, we will surely be persecuted on many levels. Get used to it. The good news is that God has grace to get us through *and* He wastes nothing! This causes great joy for me and resonates deeply in my heart, and no one and nothing can take it away from me no matter how much they try to steal it.

Today, count it all joy when trials come, and put it in the enemy's face! You are a child of the King!

But store up for yourselves treasures in heaven, where neither moth nor rust destroys, and where thieves do not break in or steal; for where your treasure is, there your heart will be also.

— MATTHEW 6:20-21

DECEMBER 27

"My heart cannot be bound"

No matter how hard the world tries to steal our joy or

rob us of our victory in Christ, it cannot be done! Even if we lose our lives, the enemy cannot win! Regardless of your circumstances today, let this truth resonate deeply within your heart and mind: you cannot be bound! Even if you are poor, even if you are physically incapacitated, even if you are alone, even if you are homeless. *No matter what!* In Jesus, I am free because I know whose I am and because I know *who I am!* I am free because I am His. Because of this, I cannot be bound—ever!

You are as free as you believe you are. Walk in that freedom today.

So if the Son makes you free, you will be free indeed.

—JOHN 8:36

DECEMBER 28

"They can't conceal it"

When a heart is set free, it is free regardless of the circumstances it finds itself in. Some of the freest individuals I have ever met are in *prison!* True freedom is available regardless of how our bodies might be confined. Just ask Joni Eareckson Tada who is confined to a wheelchair yet freely paints and ministers. Just ask Helen Keller, who rose to prominence though blind and deaf. Just ask Dave Roever who was left maimed and disfigured by a phosphorus grenade yet ministers freedom and healing and hope to others. Freedom is a state of mind and a position of heart. We are free in Jesus by virtue of the blood He shed and our nature as new creations. We are free to think as new creations, and as a new creation thinks, so he is!

Think wisely today. Be free!

> Do not eat the bread of a selfish man,
>> Or desire his delicacies;
>> For as he thinks within himself, so he is.

— PROVERBS 23:6-7A

DECEMBER 29

"I will celebrate the goodness of the Lord"

Celebration is an expression of joy over something good that has come your way. Our new identity in Christ is cause for continual celebration! God's ability to take even what the enemy means for evil and use it for good is cause for ongoing celebration! Our God-given ability to see from the King's perspective is cause for great and continuous celebration! When you think about it, *now* is the time for celebration!

Regardless of your circumstances or feelings today, spend time celebrating God's presence in your life by actively and outwardly expressing joy in attitude, word, or action, or all three!

> Consider it all joy, my brethren, when you encounter various trials, knowing that the testing of your faith produces endurance. And let endurance have its perfect result, so that you may be perfect and complete, lacking in nothing.

— JAMES 1:2-4

"He gave His life for me yet He keeps giving more"

We often hear it said, "You can't out-give the Lord," and this is true. But what are we really saying when we utter these words? Far too often, we use them as an excuse to keep from even *trying* to give as the Lord gives. If I had this attitude in my marriage, my wife would have walked out a long time ago! From my perspective, she gives far more than I give to our relationship, but my joy is in trying to bless her more than she blesses me. When we both have this attitude, the enemy has absolutely no place to plant his lies. Even though I cannot out-give God, I want to try! Even though I cannot possibly give Him all the glory due His name, I will try. Attitude is everything when it comes to such matters!

Let your attitude be one of gratitude today, and give as you have been given to.

Give, and it will be given to you. They will pour into your lap a good measure—pressed down, shaken together, and running over. For by your standard of measure it will be measured to you in return.

— LUKE 6:38

"O Lord, I celebrate Your goodness!"

Since this is the last day of the year, let us spend time celebrating God's goodness. Take time to sit down and make a list of all the blessings you have received over this year. One by one, thank God for each blessing. Take time to thank the people who have blessed you. Take time to thank your spouse for loving you. Take time to tell your children how much of a blessing they are to your life. Celebrate God's goodness as you close this year. Give thanks.

Oh give thanks to the Lord, for He is good,
  For His lovingkindness is everlasting.

— PSALM 107:1

BECOME A DJ INSIDER

Would you like to receive updates, special offers, and free music from me? By joining my newsletter, you'll receive all this and more.

Visit www.dennisjernigan.com/newsletter to sign up!

DISCOGRAPHY

From The Dennis Jernigan Collection

- At The Name Of Jesus

From *The Worshipper's Collection Vol. 2*

- Blessed Be The Name Of The Lord
- Holy Spirit, Come
- I Delight In You
- I Throw My Heart To The Wind
- I Will Celebrate The Goodness Of The Lord
- Take Me There
- You Are My God

From *The Worshipper's Collection Vol. 3*

- Great is Your Faithfulness
- You Come Raining

From *We Are The Army*

- But As For Me
- I Trust In Thee
- In The Shadow Of Thy Wings
- Not Even Death
- Praise Him In The Heavens
- Servants Of The Most High God
- The World's Mistaken
- We Are The Army
- What Time I Am Afraid

WHO IS DENNIS JERNIGAN?

Dennis Jernigan is a Kingdom Seeker. On November 7, 1981 he walked out of his old identity and into the Kingdom of God. He began to seek Jesus—the King—and not a ministry, yet ministry has flowed out of his life in world-reaching ways. His songs are sung in tens of thousands of churches around the world each and every week. His story is read and heard and recounted to thousands each month via YouTube, Facebook, dennisjernigan.com, and his many speaking and concert engagements.

Through the years, Dennis has been privileged to work with the likes of Dr. James Dobson, Steve Farrar, Anne Graham Lotz, James Robison, Beth Moore, Max Lucado, and Andy Comiskey and has recorded with Annie Herring,

Matthew Ward, Alvin Slaughter, Rebecca St. James, Travis Cottrell, Charlie Hall, Natalie Grant, Ron Kenoly, Christie Nockels, First Call, and Twila Paris.

Dennis Jernigan's mission statement can be boiled down to this:

> The Spirit of the Lord is upon me, because he anointed me to preach the gospel to the poor. He has sent me to proclaim release to the captives, and recovery of sight to the blind, to set free those who are oppressed, to proclaim the favorable year of the Lord.
>
> — LUKE 4:18-19

Dennis lives with his wife, Melinda, in Muskogee, OK, where they raised their nine children. They are now welcoming many grandchildren.

To book Dennis Jernigan for ministry, call 918-781-1200 or simply email us at mail@dennisjernigan.com.

For more information:
www.dennisjernigan.com
mail@dennisjernigan.com
patreon.com/dennisjernigan

facebook.com/official.dennisjernigan

youtube.com/dennisjernigan

instagram.com/dennisjernigan

twitter.com/dennisjernigan

amazon.com/author/dennisjernigan

CPSIA information can be obtained
at www.ICGtesting.com
Printed in the USA
LVHW010317100720
660306LV00018B/1356